REAL MEN RAISE
THEIR KIDS

REAL MEN RAISE THEIR KIDS

Matthew W. Koven

iUniverse, Inc.

New York Lincoln Shanghai

REAL MEN RAISE THEIR KIDS

iUniverse, Inc.

For information address:
iUniverse, Inc.
2021 Pine Lake Road, Suite 100
Lincoln, NE 68512
www.iuniverse.com

ISBN: 0-595-33216-1 (pbk)
ISBN: 0-595-66776-7 (cloth)

Printed in the United States of America

This book is dedicated to my loving father, mother, and brother. May our memories and love last forever.

"By the time a man realizes that maybe his father was right, he usually has a son who thinks he's wrong."

—Charles Wadsworth

"It is a wise father that knows his own child"

—William Shakespeare

Contents

Acknowledgments

I would like to thank:

My mother for her thoughts and input.

My brother and best friend for his help and support.

Ann Fisher for her professional advice

Coach Hamling and Coach Freed for their invaluable inspiration.

Introduction

As a junior in high school, I am constantly interacting with the many different products of parents' ideas, habits, lessons, values, morals, and characteristics. Parents raise their kids in diverse ways, which is responsible for the variety of kids that I am among each day.

These days it is very common, for a mother to do the majority of the child rearing job because the father is too busy working and cannot afford the extra time to spend with the kids. And because so many women have high-ranking career positions, it is not unusual for both parents to be working full time jobs, which leaves the kids vulnerable to the influence of, say, a full time nanny or whoever is hired to help raise them. Farther along the spectrum, is the "house Dad." This condition is created when the mother travels to work every day, but the father stays at home to simultaneously work at home, run errands, cook dinner most of the time, and spend time with the kids. This last condition is not the exact environment that I grew up within, but it comes close.

I, the proud son of Mr. and Mrs. Robert Koven, have had a unique childhood experience. Dad has had a tremendous influence in the molding of my character and personality. If there is one common saying that could be affiliated with Dad it is that "Shit happens." For some strange reason, Dad always gets caught in the middle of ridiculous situations. Although most of these situations could be handled in an intelligent manner, the character of Dad will not allow it. His response to the common stressful situation is unlike most, and many members of society would probably vote to place him in a zoo if possible. Nonetheless, Dad has given me countless memorable experiences and an unforgettable childhood. On the other hand, Mom should not be forgotten. She also works day in and day out constantly looking out for her two sons, tirelessly getting up at five a.m. every morning and not going to bed until eleven just to make sure that the household runs smoothly. When emotions run high between other members of the family, she acts as the mediator and brings everyone back together. She truly breathes every day just for the happiness of her family and if she were not here, the family would surely have a much harder time surviving. Both she and my older brother bring different traits to the table that constantly keep our lives in balance. Sometimes when one person is acting in bad character it will bring out the best in someone else. It is a constant cycle that will continue until the day we die.

The following manuscript contains many shocking events that may begin to paint a false image of my father's character. The stories that I have chosen to write about in this book represent only a fraction of the true being of my father. A chaotic and stressful situation has its own unique effect for each person, and Dad's reaction to most of these situations is by simply adding more commotion. However, in reality Dad is one of the kindest men that you could possibly ever meet. He is always there when anyone in the family needs him. He constantly supports Bobby and I in anything that we undertake, yet holds us back from doing anything that we should not be doing. With my father as one of our guides through life, we have grown up with morals and ethics, knowing right from wrong, and trying to learn every possible aspect of life. He makes sure that we take no shortcuts in life and push ourselves to the limit. I can honestly and proudly say that I would be simply lost without him.

The stories in this book represent some of the most memorable times of my life and I can only pray that they continue onward; however, if I were to die tomorrow, I would most certainly die happy.

1

Anger Management

To fully understand Robert Koven requires an understanding of his abnormally short temper and his general lack of patience, for it is this attribute that has generated the colorful events of my youth. This double-edged gift presents itself on a routine daily basis, whether he is preparing the perfect meal, settling bills with maintenance men (or more likely trying to fix a problem without the maintenance man) or, of course, trying to fix that "goddamn, mother-fucking cable television that isn't worth a goddamn penny!" Besides numerous daily opportunities to lose his cool, most of the events that happen throughout the day push Dad's temper to its full capacity.

Settling Confrontations
(Usually After Starting Them)

Growing up in western Kentucky, Dad understands that there is no way to settle an argument that does not require a .357 magnum. As one can imagine, this causes multiple problems (usually for the other person). I clearly remember times while barreling down the road in the Chevy Suburban, when Dad would exclaim, "That son-of-a-bitch just cut me off!" Following the conspired cut-off, we promptly approach the offender, exchange many forms of sign, body, and other languages, and at the peak of the road rage, draw the Smith and Wesson .357 magnum, thereby casting the deciding vote in the confrontation. The dispute usually ends with the opposing vehicle rapidly departing in some fashion, whether by suddenly leaving the road via an exit ramp or the emergency lane, or by vastly increasing the distance between the two vehicles. I still cannot understand why no other person has adopted this solution to arguments and taken Dad up on the challenge; however, I am glad this has not happened because being from Kentucky, he is a "damn good shot."

Although his behavior is rash, it has endowed me with the ability to learn "how to get things done!" For example, if you have to wait for the power company to restore your electricity when an ice storm knocks it out, then you should try Dad's patented Kentucky hillbilly tactic to ensure that the power company will restore your electricity before restoring it to the rest of your neighborhood. In the early winter of 2002, my family and the rest of Georgia south of the Piedmont region, experienced an ice storm that enveloped power lines with two inches of snapping icicles. Most of Atlanta and its suburbs had no power for days. This not only posed a problem for most Atlantans, it posed an even greater problem for the Kovens. Living off a main road and not in a major subdivision, our power would be fixed last, after the surrounding neighborhoods and subdivision were brought on line. Although this fact seemed logical to most rational people, Mr. Koven was convinced otherwise. Dad next spent hours on his cell phone arguing with a girl named Staci at Cobb County EMC about having our power restored. After having been told that it would take several days for our power to return, Dad decided to fix the problem himself. To do this, he reverted to the flawless "Kentucky problem-solving method." After cursing profusely about having burned coal that generated two times more BTU's than wood, Dad finally resorted to force. With pistol in hand, he got into his Suburban and swiftly traveled to Cobb County EMC. The first person that Dad encountered on his mission was a secretary with a name tag that read "Staci," who was sitting in the main office of Cobb EMC. After noticing Dad's obvious state of distress, Staci asked, "May I help you, sir?"

"Yes!" Dad screamed as he noticed the name tag. "You can help me by going out to one of your little service trucks, placing your fat ass in the driver's seat, and drive five miles to my house to fix the goddamn power!" Then he walked past her and into the manager's office. Staci was so shocked by his comment that she did not even bother calling after him. He proceeded into the manager's office with the handy-dandy .357 anything but concealed. Dad stood in front of the manager, who was quickly trying to end a conference call. The manager, a nimble man with extremely stained teeth from office coffee and cheap cigarettes, was on the phone. The CB radio that allowed the manager to communicate with his technicians whined in the background.

"How can I help, sir?" asked the manager after hanging up the phone. He had a cocky car salesmen voice.

"First, my name is Robert Koven and I believe I have spoken with you several times on the phone concerning the repair of my power."

The manager held out his hand to shake, but Dad did not reciprocate.

The manager's voice now sounded shaky. "Yes, I remember speaking with you and explaining that your power will be fixed in a matter of days. However, we must restore power to the larger communities in this part of the county first." The manager was not only nervous, but he was probably also astonished that one of the many faceless customers that he spoke lies to every day had come to see him in person, not to mention accompanied by a weapon.

"Well sir, would it be too much trouble to have one of your trucks stop by my house on its way to a larger neighborhood? I live near The Atlanta Country Club and I understand that their power is down too," Dad said politely.

Gazing down the entire time, the manager quickly said, "I am really sorry, but we cannot afford to get behind schedule over a single resident."

"Wait a minute, goddamn it! Now you listen to me for one goddamn minute!" Dad screamed as he placed the threatening .375 magnum on the manager's desk.

"Now just calm down. There is no need to get upset," the manager began to say. Then he glanced at the pistol on his desk and up at Dad. "Mr. Koven, I am truly sorry for the inconvenience that you and your family have experienced, and I will have a repair crew sent out to your place to fix the power by the end of the day if that is a satisfactory solution for you."

"I think that is an adequate solution and I do appreciate the service; however, in the future, I expect better service the first time I ask for it." Dad picked up the pistol and turned to leave. As he was walking out of the office door he said, "Just remember that the customer comes first." Just as Dad finished making his last comment, he turned and walked right into the eavesdropping Staci, who had been leaning against the office door and listening to the conversation. After saying, "excuse me" to her, Dad left the building and came home. I am proud to say that to this day, whenever there is a power outage, the Kovens' residence is always fixed before the end of that day.

Chef Koven

One prerequisite to be the quintessential "house Dad" is the ability to cook amazing meals. My father made sure that his kids would grow up having tasted everything on the food spectrum. Bobby and I were eating sushi shortly after we learned to walk. He cooks restaurant-quality meals, prepares exotic and new foods that one usually would never fathom sampling, and of course, he is psychotic throughout the entire process of preparing his gourmet meals.

It was a beautiful New Year's Day while staying in one of our family friends' vacation home located outside of Scottsdale, Arizona. The Kovens were very close to the Keeters, and when they graciously invited us to Arizona for a New Year celebration, we happily accepted. Spending close to a week in Arizona for a holiday usually consisted of non-stop golf for the men, a marathon of shopping for the women, and a useless desert to make use of by the kids. Although the desert turned out to be not so useless, the Keeter's daughter, Kaylan, Bobby, and I always found something to do. However, by dinner time, Dad would be completely drained of any motivation to do anything. We planned to celebrate New Year's Day with a large family dinner at the house that Chef Koven had offered to prepare. While standing on the patio, Dad turned to Julie Keeter, and said, "Julie, have you ever tasted my famous trout almandine?"

"You know Bob, I don't think that I've tried that dish before, but I've heard it is spectacular," Julie said.

Dad interrupted with, "Julie, spectacular is not a strong enough word to describe it. It's out of this world, and by god you are in for a treat! I know that you wanted to go out to a restaurant for New Year's Day, but there's nobody that can make trout almandine better than I can. See, I have this special sauce that"

Mom interrupted him. "Robert! Quit boring Julie with your cooking jabber. We all know that we will be drilled on the subject when dinner is served."

"Julie, please excuse Gale's comments. She just doesn't understand how to prepare gourmet meals," Dad said with a chuckle.

As Dad walked back into the house, Mom turned to Julie. "If there's one piece of advice about cooking with Bob that I can offer, it's to stay the hell away from the kitchen when he's in it. I try to give him room to cook, so I leave the kitchen. Then, he calls me to ask for help. So I go back into the kitchen, but I'm always either in the way or not doing something right, so I just leave. It gets him madder than a hornet, but I swear, Julie, that the minute he sits down at the table, he does not even act like there was an argument."

"You know, Jim is the same way, and even though I like to cook, it seems to be too much of a hassle so we just decide to go out. However, when he's out of town I can cook as much as I want because there's no pressure," Julie said.

Knowing his reputation for making great meals and not really wanting to have to deal with it himself, Jim Keeter agreed that Dad should do the cooking. With this said, and knowing what the near future would bring, Bobby and I quickly rented some movies and located ourselves as far away from the kitchen as possible.

Thanks to Dad's viewing of too many cooking shows on TV, and feeling like Emeril himself, when beginning to cook, Dad expects to have all his ingredients perfectly separated into little tiny bowls, just like on TV. As Chef Koven begins to cook, thoughts of which ingredients he needs begin to fly everywhere because he has only one recipe, and that is the one in his head. On this New Year's Day, he begins by cleaning the trout, and once that's finished, starts adding spices, herbs, and other seasonings. However, a horrible thought strikes him right as he is placing the trout on the grill. He has forgotten about the black-eyed peas, rice, and other vegetables. Although all the black-eyed peas and other side dishes had already been taken care of by Julie Keeter, they were not taken care of by Chef Koven. What if the vegetables and rice were not up to par with the trout? This would mean that the level of appreciation given to him for the exceptionable trout would be reduced, and the meal would be less than perfect. This inconceivable thought unleashes a landslide of emotions, mostly negative, that envelope the entire kitchen and whoever is in it. Dad walks over to the simmering peas, grabs a spoon, and takes a sample. His facial expression changes to distraught as he begins to fumble through a rack of spices. "Julie do you have onion powder, not onion salt?"

"Yes, I do, but Gale already added it to the peas," Julie says sweetly.

Dad gives her a concerned look. "Well, I think…. No, I'm positive that it needs more onion powder. It's not quite right.

"I'm pretty sure Gale put quite a bit of that onion powder in the peas. I mean, I really don't think that it needs more, but if you insist, I will get it for you," Julie said, irritated. This comment appeared to cause Dad further frustration. Any time his exceptional cooking skills are challenged in any way, he labels the comment or challenge as enemy and proceeds to destroy its ability to exist.

With sweat already beginning to bead on Dad's cheeks and forehead, he said, "Julie, the correct amount of onion powder is essential to this dish. Do you not agree?"

"Why yes, I do," she replied with a confused look.

"And do you agree that after adding onion powder to the peas that it creates a slight sour, but not too sour a taste?" Dad asked.

"Well, I guess so," said Julie.

"And because the trout almandine has a sweet taste, there must be a dish, the black-eyed peas, which will slightly neutralize the sweet taste and produce a splendid experience. That is why the extra onion powder is completely necessary and that is why it is also necessary that I am the one cooking and you are the one fetching the onion powder," Dad said in an unyielding voice.

As Julie slammed the onion powder down upon the countertop, she said, "Well, if you need your sou-chef, she will be in the den."

As soon as Julie sat down on the sofa, Jim said, "Now Juleeeeee, you know you shouldn't have gone in there and bothered Bob. Gale told me that she gave you a preemptive warning."

Julie sighed with resignation, picked up a book and retired to the patio.

Although Bobby and I had located ourselves in a room that was as far away from the kitchen as possible, the commotion was loud and clear, and we both gave each other unsurprised looks. "There goes the Cooking Nazi again," Bobby said.

"Yeah, you know it's never a perfect meal unless someone gets crucified during the process of preparing it," I said with a laugh.

Once the challenge of cooking was finally finished, the meal was served. One would think that after such a challenge, Mr. Koven would barely have the energy to eat. Instead, Dad might as well print out a written survey on each item of the meal, with background information on every detail that went into the cooking process. This is because soon after the non-existent prayer that starts the meal, everyone is flooded with questions such as, "Isn't the trout great? How do you like it? This is the absolute best trout money can buy. Do you taste the spice? That's what makes this dish complete because if I had not added lemon pepper and those chopped almonds....." On and on and on. I feel like I am being polled for a food-tasting contest. Although it is a challenge for everybody, the food is usually great and by the time the meal is halfway done, real conversation takes the place of food conversation and everybody does enjoy and appreciate Dad's hard work.

My First Lesson in Thinking

Ever since I can remember, Dad's creed has been: "Shoot first and ask questions later!" and at the same time: "Think before you act." I often wondered how it was possible to abide by both mottos simultaneously. But it did not really matter because Dad always knew and had no problem letting me know.

It was a beautiful morning and I was more excited than I had ever been in all the previous five years of my hayseed childhood. A morning like this one usually began with Dad yelling at the top of his lungs, "Get the hell up! We're late!" Although the morning of a hunting day was the only type of morning that Dad was able to wake up on time for, we still always managed to be late. Bobby and I would usually wake up later than Dad; yet, we would still get dressed, have the car packed, and be ready to go before Dad was even dressed. Mom always had breakfast waiting for us when we were supposes to leave; however, her famous buckwheat pancakes were not always the best food for the stomach, especially on a day like this one. Dad would always tell me, "Now don't eat too many of those cakes or else you'll be shitting like a goose for the rest of the day." Although he would quickly eat the extra pancakes that I had abstained from, I figured that a dove field would not be the best place to be "shitting like a goose."

After our hastily eaten breakfast, we would all pile in to the loaded down Chevrolet Suburban and drive to Cartersville, Georgia where we would meet our friends at the local McDonald's. It was the same routine every year: Mr. Timothy Harris, one of Dad's friends, would say, "How y'all doin' today?"

"Not to damn good," Dad would answer. And just like the previous year, Dad said, "I don't know, Tim, I drove out here yesterday around five o' clock to scout the fields, and not one bird was in the air."

"You old fart. You say that every year, and we always manage to do fine," said Tim Harris.

"All I can say is that if it were not for me driving out here the day before the hunt every year, we would not even have a spot on the field," Dad said.

"And if were not for me, we would not even have tickets to get into the hunt," said Tim Harris.

The dove hunt that we were going to attend that day was a distinguished one called The Governor's Hunt. It took place on a large plantation or farm, where all the guests attend a large barbecue on the property before the hunt officially begins. The barbecue consisted of a large group of hunters that did nothing but stand around and gorge themselves with complimentary beer, coke, cheese, and barbecue that resulted in such intense heartburn and indigestion that most of the people there wanted to do anything but hunt by the time the event began. However, it was a nice gathering and to make the day even more enjoyable, the Governor would arrive and speak for about twenty minutes.

As we were in the process of leaving McDonalds and walking toward our automobiles, Tim Harris suddenly said, "Wait a minute, Bob. I almost forgot to give you your tickets for the hunt." As Tim Harris fumbled through a worn envelope that contained the tickets, and realized that there was one left after he had taken his ticket and given us our tickets. As he picked up the remaining ticket, he read the name, "Doug Warwick." Doug Warwick was friend of both Dad and Tim Harris, who had hunted with us at all of the Governor's Hunts in the past. Tim Harris turned to Dad. "Did you not call Doug last night and tell him that I had a ticket for him this year?"

As a look of horror came over Dad's face, he said, "Tim, I thought that you had already told him. Don't tell me that you never told him."

"Jesus Christ," Tim Harris said with a sigh. "I didn't even notice that he was not here to meet us. I feel terrible."

"Me, too," Dad said. "Well, it's only ten o' clock. Maybe if I give him a call, he can get here within the next couple of hours. As Dad telephoned Doug, we piled back into the Suburban and drove toward the farm that was located about three miles down the road.

After having listened to the governor speak and having dodged the greasy barbecue, my excitement was growing. Not only because it was opening day of dove season in Georgia, but because I had just received my first shotgun, which also meant that this time I would actually be able to shoot and not just act as the "bird boy," the youngest child on the dove field who is responsible for retrieving the dead birds. I was too young to sit by myself camouflaged amidst the tall cornstalks of the dove field, but I still felt powerful. The smell of freshly ignited gunpowder was in the air and I was more than ready to test out the sleek single-shot 410-gauge shotgun.

As soon as lunch was over we headed toward the dove field. And that's when we saw Doug Warwick's pickup truck driving in the opposite direction. As Dad flagged him down with his hand, both automobiles came to a stop next to each other along the side of the road.

"Where in the hell have you been?" Dad's tone was joking.

"Well, if I had known where in the hell I was supposed to have been, it might have helped," Doug replied in a friendly voice.

"Doug, I am really damn sorry about this fiasco, but if it makes you feel any better, we have the best damn spot in the field because I came up here yesterday and scouted the place out," Dad chirped.

"Sounds like a plan," Doug replied as he let his foot off the brake and began to turn around behind us.

When we finally made it to the field, I found my position and sat down on my hunting stool ready for action. However, most other hunters were in the process of congregating in small groups around the outskirts of the field. Moreover, Dad's congregation of friends was unlike the rest of the small camouflaged groups. His group was much easier to pick out, mainly because they did not take care to stand near or under any type of cover that would inhibit their ability to be seen.

"So you finally decided to give ole Matt a chance this year," Tim Harris said.

"Well, the little devil is finally growing up, and it's about time that he starts taking a few shots of his own, instead of constantly picking up birds for your lazy ass. Anyway, look at him. He looks like a little damn professional," Dad said proudly.

"Just wait until he starts driving and asking for money. Then we'll see how happy you are about having him," Tim Harris said as he joyfully cut a fart in front of the rest of the men.

The dove shoot progressed slowly through the hot September afternoon. As soon as Dad had joined me, he proceeded to shoot every one of the four doves that tried to light in the field. Suddenly, I noticed a group of doves flying toward us. I directed Dad's attention to the birds and he signaled for me to fire. As I cocked the hammer back, I realized that since I was two feet shorter than my father, and since the birds' flight pattern crossed the back of his head, if I shot, the projectile would explode out of the barrel next to Dad's head. Remembering the "Think before you act" motto, I hesitated; however, I had forgotten my expected knowledge of the "Shoot and ask questions later" motto. Dad, seeing my hesitation, suddenly exploded. "Shoot, Goddamnit!" So I shot, projecting hundreds of BB's and a small, but intense explosion within inches of his ear. The chaos that followed this moment produced a noise louder than my gunshot.

Looking as if I had tried to kill him, Dad quickly snatched my treasured gift. Parting with the new shooter was like saying good-bye to a lifelong friend, even if I had only had it in my possession for a few days. The reprimanding words that followed revised my knowledge of the adult language and contained everything from "Jesus fucking Christ," "shit it in a bucket," to the estimated value of my carcass. As the string of invectives continued, I could here the muffled laughter of the other hunters who were camouflaged randomly around the field. Although I did not really understand what Dad said, I knew he was angry, so from that day forward, I began learning the art of keeping the "Shoot first…" motto and the "Think before you act" motto harmoniously balanced.

2

Putting Your Kids through School the Right Way

As early as the 3rd grade, Dad would burn the idea that "nothing but straight A's is acceptable" and that we must "be perfect" even though he was not. Well, that was the point and it worked. I have yet to make straight A's but once; however, I have never made less than a B, and usually have more A's than B's. If it was not for Dad's constant coaxing and kicking me in the ass, I really don't think that I would be nearly as good a student as I am today. I guarantee that Bobby, now attending Dartmouth College, would say the same.

Riding to School

In order to give us the best possible education, my parents decided to send me and Bobby to a private school located in College Park, Georgia. Not only is Woodward Academy located in possibly one of the roughest areas of Atlanta, it was also a grueling 45 to 60 minute, one-way commute every day, depending on traffic.

Every year before school even started, football practice began weeks in advance. In other words, if you were not old enough to drive, you had to find a way to get your ass thirty miles south with or without your parents. Because of this problem, carpools were created to save parents time. Fulfilling his out-of-office duty, Dad was always the driver of Bobby's football carpool. It consisted of about six kids, not including me, who loved Dad for his non-parental behavior. On one of the lucky carpool days, I decided to accompany Dad down to Woodward to bring the guys home. Leaving the house fifteen minutes late, which was considered perfect timing, we headed south on I-75. Once reaching College Park, Dad thought of the nice gesture to pick up some hamburgers for the guys. We quickly turned off the road and drove into the driveway for the pickup window at Checkers. When we came to the menu and the ordering box, a female voice quickly exploded, "Welcome to Checkers. May I take your order?"

"Yes, I would like six regular hamburgers, one double cheeseburger, and two chili dogs with cheese," replied Dad.

"Would like anything to drink with that?" the loud voice rapidly asked.

Dad thought for a second and with an intuitive expression on his face he said, "Give me one water, seven small cokes, and one diet coke."

"Alright, so you want six double cheeseburgers, two regulars, a chili cheese dog, one water, seven diet cokes, and one small regular coke," said the voice.

"No, No, No! I want six regular hamburgers, one double cheeseburger, and two chili dogs with cheese," Dad screamed.

"Calm down, sir. I'm just tryin' to take your order," she replied.

"And I'm just trying to give it to you," Dad said.

After another fifteen minutes of translating/screaming, the order was filled and we were on our way to school, averaging twice the legal speed limit. As we headed down a straight road, we approached an intersection. The stoplight at the intersection began to blush, but neither of us saw it nor cared to see it at that moment, so we continued onward. As we got closer, I noticed from the corner of my eye that another car was also approaching the intersection at a high speed. As the other car entered the soon-to-be danger zone, it stopped as a result of the driver freezing when she noticed a two and a half ton Suburban advancing rapidly toward her.

Dad yelled, "Hold on!" even though I had already been holding on for the past thirty minutes, and as we T-boned the Toyota Camry, I gained a better understanding of the laws of physics.

Once all of the action stopped, Dad looked at me and asked, "Are you alright?"

"Yes I'm fine; however, your chili dog didn't make it," I said as I began to unbuckle my seatbelt/chili dog and look around at the scene. Dad quickly stepped out of the car to view the damage created.

"Well, I'll be damned! Matt, there's not a scratch on the car," he said with surprise.

"That's amazing because that lady's car is completely totaled," I said, looking in the direction of the destroyed Camry. As Dad began to walk toward the vehicle, the young woman stepped out and began to survey the immense damage.

"Are you okay?" Dad asked.

"Yes, I think I'm alright, just a little banged up, that's all," she said in a disturbing voice.

"Thank God! You know, I'm not sure exactly what happened. I mean, I was running the yellow light and then you came out of nowhere," Dad said.

"Well, if you had not been going quite so fast, we probably wouldn't be in this situation. Would we?" the woman asked.

"Whatever, lady. Listen, I really do wish I could stay and argue, but I have to go pick up my kid. So here is my insurance and personal information. Dad handed her a piece of paper and stepped back into the Suburban.

"Aren't you going to wait for the police to show up?" she asked.

"Why? Listen, if they want to give me a ticket, tell them to send it to me. Otherwise, you can tell them to fuck off!" Dad was already starting the car and shifting it into drive. We drove off leaving the woman standing next to her wrecked car with an astonished look on her face. "I really hate people that can't get out of their own goddamn way," Dad exclaimed as we resumed our previous speed.

Bobby was standing outside the football stadium with his friends waiting to give Dad a piece of his mind for being an hour late, but he truly picked the wrong day. "Where have you guys been?" Bobby sounded upset.

"Where have we been?" repeated an angry Dad.

"Yeah, we've been sitting here for an hour."

"Listen, you ungrateful little fuck! I hurried down to this goddamn worthless school so fast in order to pick your ass up that Matt and I got in a fucking car accident. Now get in the goddamn car and shut the hell up!" Bobby and his shocked friends quickly loaded into the Suburban.

"You know that if you could ever learn how to leave on time" Bobby said as Dad interrupted him.

"We had left on time, but we had to fight goddamn Atlanta traffic to get here."

"Well, Mr. Koven, it doesn't look like you had a wreck. I mean, wouldn't there be dents or something?" said Fletcher, one of Bobby's friends who believed Dad's claim of having an accident to be false.

"Fletcher, do you want to walk home today?"

"Well, not particularly. I think I would rather stay for the ride and enjoy your company," Fletcher said with a grin.

"Good, now maybe you can be quiet and teach Bobby something."

Eventually, the argument did come to a stop and as I looked back, I noticed the expressions of fear on the other kids' faces. I decided to hand the hamburgers out, thinking that food might lighten up the situation. After everyone had taken one, there was still one left over. One of the boys said, "Mr. Koven, there's one hamburger left."

"There better fuckin' not be. I bought one hamburger for each person. Now, who's the asshole that didn't eat the goddamn thing after I had a wreck to buy them?" Dad shouted.

For a while no one answered, but finally, one of the boys said, "Scott didn't eat it," knowing that Scott was sick and did not come to practice that day.

Dad rapidly erupted, "Scott! If you don't eat that goddamn hamburger, I am going to shove it right up your ass!"

Finally, Bobby said, "Dad. Scott's not even here." This statement was followed by a long sequence of laughing. Eventually, Dad calmed down, and everyone in the car was in good spirits again. Many of the boys in that original car pool still enjoy recalling the day that they were able to view Mr. Koven's loving, parental confrontation with my brother.

Selecting Classes the Koven Way

When the time comes to select which students will enroll in which classes, many private schools let the teacher decide where their student shall be placed for the following year. Woodruff Academy uses this method for placing students. Although Woodruff's motto is: "Every Opportunity for Every Student," one can see that if your teacher tells you that you can only enroll into a certain class and not a different class due to your performance in the classroom, this determination does not give every student every opportunity. This flaw in Woodruff's selection system was quickly brought to the administration's attention after Bobby was not placed in the AP class that he expected to enroll in during the following year.

Even though Bobby had met the first two requirements for enrollment in AP English, his teacher, Mrs. Tubblesworth, would not allow such a thing to happen. He had fulfilled the academic requirements, as well as the PSAT requirement. However, he had not fulfilled the teacher's subjective requirement. Mrs. Tubblesworth did not see Bobby as AP material and, as acting head of the English department, she had the ultimate decision. After receiving the bad news, Bobby confronted Mrs. Tubblesworth hoping to remedy the situation. Following a school day, Bobby proceeded into Mrs. Tubblesworth's classroom.

"Hi, Mrs. Tubblesworth. I would like to discuss your recommendation for my placement next year."

"I think I recommended you for Honors English Three. Is there a problem?" she asked.

"Yes, there is a problem, because quite frankly, I do not agree with your recommendation," My brother sounded sternly.

"Well, Bobby, you understand that these recommendations are for the teacher to make, not the student. If I felt that your performance in my class was at the Advanced Placement English level, I would have recommended you for Advanced Placement English," she said briskly.

"Well, would you mind informing me of exactly how you evaluate students like myself in order to make your decision on where to place us?" Bobby asked.

"There are three categories that a student must fulfill: PSAT scores, semester grades, and a personal recommendation. You fulfilled the first two; however, as I explained juts a minute ago, I do not feel that your work in my class has been Advanced Placement material," Mrs. Tubblesworth said.

"To be honest Mrs. Tubblesworth, I do not think that your inability to give me a sufficient recommendation should be enough to override my fulfillment of the first two categories. I would greatly appreciate your re-evaluation of me as a student or some other means that can be worked out in order for you to place me into the Advanced Placement English class," Bobby said firmly.

"Mr. Koven! Are you hard of hearing? I believe that I have made it clear that you are not of the Advanced Placement level in English at Woodruff Academy. As the head of the English department I have sole oversight on who will and will not enter Advanced Placement English courses. If you do not like my policy, you can either find another high school to attend, or not graduate. Now please, leave before you anger me further," Mrs. Tubblesworth said.

"Mrs. Tubblesworth, if anyone is hard of hearing, it is you, you ignorant post-menopausal bitch! I'm not quite sure if you are aware of it, but you are in the process of ruining my life. I have worked too long and hard at this school in order to graduate having taken the most challenging curriculum with the hope of admittance to an Ivy League college. I will not allow you or anyone else to simply screw up my plans due to their failure to like me as a student. Although you may not like me as a person, I have put forth effort in your class and I have made the required grades and scores to be placed in AP English. You will be hearing from my parents as well as the principal on this matter. Have a nice day!" with that Bobby stormed out of the classroom.

When he arrived home, he told Mom about the dilemma. Although an issue like this usually demands the mobilization of a force that only Dad yields, he was out of town and Mom, who is perfectly capable of taking care such situations, was forced to deal with the matter. She quickly decided to set up a meeting with the principal to discuss the issue. Mom called Mr. Tingleberry, the principal, and he more than happy to meet with her the next day.

Mr. Tingleberry's office was a typical high school principal's office, filled with self-gratifying objects such as his graduation robe, a desk plaque that read "Principal Tim Tingleberry," and a wooden box full of detention slips that reminded him of his unlimited power over pre-disciplined students.

Mom walked confidently into his office, and said, "Hi, Mr. Tingleberry. I'm Gale Koven, Bobby Koven's mother."

"Yes, Mrs. Koven. It's a pleasure to meet you. Please, take a seat." Mr.

Tingleberry gestured toward one of the chairs in front of his desk.

As Mom took a seat in front of his desk she began the discussion with, "Mr. Tingleberry I think that you and I can both agree that the situation between my son and Mrs. Tubblesworth is quite arbitrary in the sense that Bobby is fully qualified to be placed in Advanced Placement English."

"Well, you see, Mrs. Koven, here at Woodruff Academy grades are simply not the only factor in terms of a 'qualified' student, if you will. Here we believe character to be tantamount to the importance of grades," Mr. Tingleberry said with great assurance.

Mom's eyes widened. "Well that's complete nonsense. You cannot simply deny a student opportunity due to a teacher not believing that he has enough character. I mean, at least the grades are cold facts whereas the belief of whether a person has character or not is subject to the opinion of the teacher or whoever might be evaluating the person."

"Mrs. Koven, our teachers are fully qualified for the positions they hold especially Mrs. Tubblesworth who has been with us for more than twenty five years. She has seen hundreds of students and is quite capable of evaluating them."

"Are you saying that it is impossible for the teacher to be wrong?"

"Let me just say that it is highly unlikely that our teachers are wrong in their evaluations of their students. The teachers have spent nine months with the kids."

"Well, what if a teacher "is" wrong?" Mom asked, trying to remain polite.

An uncomfortable silence enveloped the room and was finally broken by Mr. Tingleberry. "You are absolutely right. What if the teacher is wrong?" he said, even though he was thinking to himself that a teacher is never wrong when it is their word against a student. "But please remember that the teacher has spent an entire school year with the students, and she is probably the best person to decide where each student should be placed based on their capabilities and performance in the class."

Mom gave it one last try. "Why can't each student decide where he or she would like to be placed, and if they fail because of their ignorant decision, they can drop out or continue to fail? It will then be the student's fault and not the teacher's bad decision. However, if you tell a student that he cannot participate in classes that he may have otherwise succeeded in, you are only denying him a learning opportunity."

Tingleberry, now looking very frustrated, finally said, "Mrs. Koven, I do not believe that you fully understand how we operate here at Woodruff Academy. We specifically look for which of the academically achieved students have the potential to attend Ivy League colleges and other top universities, and then begin to help those students, which usually consist of about five exemplary kids. Those students will receive the department awards; they will receive the desired placements, the best recommendations, and the best of everything else that we have to offer. If your student lies outside of this group, he obviously does not have as high a caliber of mind, therefore, will be cut out of these benefits. Do you now understand why your son was not placed in Advanced Placement English, Mrs. Koven?"

Mom, now about to fall out of her chair, replied angrily, "No, I do not. I think children and their parents should be allowed to decide their own fate! This isn't a place for learning, it's a place for controlling the fate of people we like and people we do not like!" she quickly exited Tingleberry's office and the building.

Once home, and feeling as if she lost the battle, but not the war, Mom decided to call Dad, who was attending a golf tournament. She explained what had happened and Dad became enraged. Because a principal of all people had upset Mom, Dad blew a gasket. It was no longer a problem of getting Bobby into the English class; instead, it became a challenge of how much Dad could scare or threaten Tim Tingleberry.

As always, it begins with a polite, yet intense message that is left on the victim's office phone. Once the message is not returned within forty-eight hours, Dad leaves a second message that is less polite and more intense. Most people respond readily after this second message, however, Tingleberry did not. Feeling that someone has directly challenged his authority on matters that included his sons, Dad made a hasty journey to Woodward. Like a bat out of hell, Dad burst through the door into Principal Tingleberry's office, with what most people would identify as a homicidal look upon his face. Tingleberry, who was on the phone, was caught completely off guard, and out of fright, slammed the phone down which ended his long distance call to his brother in Europe. Dad quickly said, "Hi Tim, I'm Bob Koven, Bobby's Dad and the husband of the lady that you, unfortunately, upset yesterday. Also, just for the record, I will be leaving this office either with your career or Bobby's improved placement. So, let's get started."

"Mr. Koven, I wasn't expecting you," said Mr. Tingleberry his voice shaking.

"Yeah, I didn't think it was necessary to call about an issue that was as concerning as this one. I figured that you would probably still be trying to get the situation resolved with Mrs. Tubblesworth," Dad said.

"Well, Bob. I hope it's alright if I call you Bob. I have spoken with Mrs. Tubblesworth and she still feels strongly about the original recommendation that she made."

"Tim, to be honest I really couldn't give two shits about what Mrs. Tubblesworth has to say on the matter. I am really interested in what your opinion is," Dad said, his eyes piercing right through Tingleberry.

"Well, I would have to say that my first inclination on this matter would be to go with what the teacher recommended. You know Bob, this teacher has spent the past nine."

"Listen, you balless sonofabitch, I don't give a fuck if Mrs. Tubblesworth has spent the past nine months with Jesus Christ! Her personal recommendation should not even stand the slightest chance of accreditation when compared with Bobby's standardized testing scores and grades. If you don't have the balls to stand up against a measly English teacher, you ought to have your ass fired because you are doing a disservice to this institution. Moreover, if you can't do your job as the principal, I will go to infinite lengths to make sure you will never be placed in a position of authority over students of any kind. I will personally guarantee to make your life a living hell. Do I make myself clear, Tim?"

Mr. Tingleberry did not budge during the entire lecture. The first expression of concern for Bobby's situation appeared on his face following Dad's harangue. "Well, I'm sorry you feel that way, Bob."

"I hope you are goddamn sorry because I expect this fucking disaster to get straightened out immediately. Also, Tim, if I have not made my point clear enough already, you should be aware that you haven't only pissed me off, but if you don't change this recommendation, then you will be drowning a kid's future dreams. Bobby has done nothing but invest time and effort into this unholy place and it seems that all you people will give in return is disappointment. I will check back with you tomorrow evening and if this isn't cleared up, your goddamn head will be on my wall!"

"Is that a threat?" asked Mr. Tingleberry.

"It's not a threat, it's a motherfuckin' promise and you better believe it! Have a nice day!" Dad shouted as he turned and left the office.

The next day, Dad telephoned Mr. Tingleberry and it was confirmed that Bobby would be placed in AP English regardless of Mrs. Tubblesworth's decision. The next year, Bobby gave a straight "A" performance in his English class, and if it had not been for Dad, Bobby would not have had the opportunity to perform so well.

3

Traveling with Dad

For most people, the word "travel" conjures images of airplanes, foreign lands, different cultures, other exciting aspects of typical voyages. However, when I think of the word "travel," images and thoughts of confrontation, confusion, unexpected happenings, and other challenging aspects of travel, come to mind. It is almost a relief when I arrive home after a long vacation, whether it was an uneventful trip or the most frenzied and chaotic excursion I have ever experienced, because either I am amazed that nothing happened or that more: did not happen. As our guide through whatever destination we travel to, Dad changes roles from the "house Dad" to whatever is needed during our unforgettable trips. Whether it is assuming the identity of the chief editor of *Cooking Light Magazine* in order to get reservations, or becoming a travel agent, Dad is always there to get us a seat in the best restaurants or a discount on the finest hotels.

Mexico: Montezuma's Revenge

In what would become the first, of many family vacations, that we took with our good friends, the Keeters, we decided to journey to Cabo San Lucas, located at the tip of the Baja Peninsula in Mexico. We arrived, feeling refreshed by the warm salty air, and continued to our hotel. After assuming the identity of a travel agent, Dad checked us into the hotel and since it was getting late, we settled quickly into our rooms and prepared to go to dinner. When we arrived at the restaurant called the giggling Marlin, there was an extremely long line of people and the wait was estimated to be over an hour. Dad decided that there was no reason that he should have to wait that long. He covertly looked at the waiting list while trying to talk to the Spanish speaking host as best as he could.

"Hola!" Dad said as he approached the hostess.

"Hola senor! Cuánta gente está en su partido?" asked the hostess.

"Uh yes. Correcto mundo. I no se espanol," Dad said as he scanned the waiting list in search of a suitable name. As soon as he spotted "Gomez" for a party of seven he had hit the jackpot. "Si, we are the Gomez party," Dad said as the hostess simply starred at him with a non-comprehending look upon her face. He turned to my brother. "Bobby! Tell this lady what in the hell is going on."

"Señora, somos el partido de Gomez para siete. Creo que tenemos reservas," Bobby said.

"Si," the hostess said with a relieved look as she turned to show us to a table.

Within the next few minutes we were seated and giving orders for drinks. The restaurant served great food and we all had superb dinners. But there was a slight problem. Dad's stomach had been giving him some trouble earlier and by the time dinner which with the Keeters, averaged three to four hours, was coming to an end, Dad was about to literally explode.

"Gale!" Dad spouted in a whisper.

"What, Bob?"

"Do you have any Tums or something in your purse? My stomach is killing me."

"I left all of that stuff back at the hotel. Is your stomach still bothering you?"

"Yeah, it must be from the water or something," he said as he grabbed the waiter who was nearby. "Senor, could you please bring us a bill as soon as possible?"

"Si, senor," said the waiter.

"Now, Bob, don't be trying to pull any sly tricks over there. You know it's my turn to pay," Mr. Keeter said as he noticed Dad talking to the waiter.

"Jim, just relax and enjoy the Mexican moonlight. Besides, I'm pretty darn sure that you picked up the last one," Dad said while uncomfortably shifting in his chair to ease the intestinal pressure building up. It wasn't too long after this that Dad noticed the waiter passing by without giving him the bill. By now the pressure was really beginning to build up. Dad quickly got the waiter's attention by grabbing his arm. "Senor! I necssita el billeta muy rapido! Capice?" Finally, as soon as the bill touched the tablecloth, Dad threw down his credit card, stood up, and headed for the bathroom. However, the credit card that Dad carelessly placed on the table was one that the restaurant did not accept. In order to correct Dad's mistake, the waiter quickly stood in front of Dad and began rapidly explaining the problem in Spanish. With only one thing on his mind, Dad screamed, "Get out of the way before I pass out!"

"Senor!" the waiter insisted as Dad pushed him out of the way and headed for the bathroom. As he approached the heavenly room, he noticed a paper sign on the door that read, "Out of order." Dad, now feeling like a bomb getting ready to detonate, undertook a jog/hop and promptly exited the restaurant leaving the Keeters and the rest of his family sitting at the table in bewilderment.

Once outside, Dad headed toward a beat-up gas station that looked like it had been last seen in a horror movie. He burst into the 5x20 food mart and went straight for the single unisex bathroom in the corner. However, Dad's bathroom flight did not end here because he was going to have a much larger problem in a few moments. After about thirty-five minutes of relieving himself, he noticed that there was no toilet paper available.

"What kind of place doesn't have toilet paper in the bathroom," he said to himself. Believe me, this would be one time in Dad's life when toilet paper would be appraised at a higher value than anything else.

So, Dad got himself together as best he could in order to move about thirty feet, and he made his way to the clerk behind the counter in the store. Using his tourist refined Spanish he said, "You no have toilet paper. I neccccita toilita paperrr muy badly. Comprende?" The clerk, knowing what he meant, but acting otherwise, just looked at him. Dad's stomach began to rumble again and soon after, his knees started to knock. Finally, Dad said, "Listen you dumb bastard! If you don't give me some goddamn toilet paper, I'm going to blow a hole through the seat of my pants!"

The clerk, trying not to laugh, said, "Five hundred pesetas" as he pulled a roll of toilet paper out from behind the counter.

Dad was astonished. "You want five hundred pesetas for toilet paper?" Then, feeling the pressure in his stomach building back up he said, "Fine, give it to me," as he shakily threw down the five hundred pesetas, while the clerk handed him approximately three feet of toilet paper. Being in too much of an emergency to protest the unfair amount, Dad ran toward the bathroom. As you can imagine, the clerk might as well have handed Dad a piece of tissue because three feet of toilet paper lasted about one stroke. Soon after, Dad was back in front of the clerk, paying another five hundred pesetas for another three feet of toilet paper. However, by the third visit to the clerk, Dad finally said, "Listen you goddamn thief, this is the last time I'm hobbling my ass out here to give you five hundred peseta for three feet of toilet paper. You can take all of my goddamn funny money; just give me the whole fucking roll!"

"No problem," the clerk said in plain English as he handed Dad the roll. Dad quickly threw all the pesetas he had toward the man and headed for the unbearable bathroom.

By the time Dad returned to the table, he looked like he had run a marathon. Sweat was beaded all over his neck and face, and he had a sweat mark down to his belt.

"Jesus, Bob. Who in the hell was chasing you?" Mr. Keeter said with a laugh.

"If anything was chasing me, it was this Mexican water in my system. I need to start drinking bottled water," Dad said.

"I though you were trying to get out of paying the bill," joked Mr. Keeter.

"I think I would try to find a less obvious way to get out of paying the bill," Dad assured him.

Shortly afterwards we all departed for the hotel. If anyone slept well that night, I would have to say that Dad probably did, especially following his aerobic exercise that evening.

Making a Good Impression

After eating large breakfasts followed by lavish dinners, it did not take long for Dad to start complaining about how bad he felt from the huge meals and absence of exercise. On one of the many late rising mornings, Dad turned to Mom and said, "Uh, my feet and ankles have gotten so swollen on this trip it's unbelievable."

"Well, honey, all that you really have to do is stop eating such large portions at breakfast and dinner. That food is so salty, it's no wonder you're retaining fluid," Mom said.

"I know. I can't take it. I feel like I'm going to have a heart attack. My blood sugar shoots up and down, my blood pressure is high, my feet and ankles are swollen, and I haven't had any exercise since we got here."

"Well, aren't you at least getting some walking in while you and Jim play golf?" Mom asked.

"Hell, no. We use the golf carts. Besides, if I have to play another goddamn round of golf, I think I might kill myself. It's hotter than a goddamn furnace out there, and on top of that Jim enjoys swinging clubs in the midst of the heat. By the time we reach the clubhouse I'm exhausted. It's all I can do to simply stuff myself with the complimentary trail mix at the bar," he complained while laying on the bed.

"You know, you really shouldn't eat that trail mix. It's very salty," Mom scolded.

"I know, goddamn it! That why I'm complaining. If I don't eat the trail mix, then my blood sugar drops and I feel like hell."

As Dad continued to complain, Bobby and I could hear every word of it through the wall of the neighboring room. "Does he ever stop bitching?" I asked.

"I don't think so. It's what he does best," Bobby said.

"Maybe it's just me, but how can his life be that hard? He has to go and play golf; what a horrible dilemma," I said.

"Yeah, but you never know. He probably does feel like shit," Bobby said.

"Maybe, but that doesn't mean he has to wake us up talking about it.,"

As Dad's complaining continued, Mom finally suggested, "Maybe you would feel better if you went to the gym. The resort has a great fitness facility."

"Maybe I'll go, but I'll still feel like hell," Dad said with disappointment. Finally, after making certain that everyone in the family knew what was wrong with him and how hard a time he was having, Dad decided to actually take a trip to the hotel's fitness facility.

Before I proceed any further with this story, I would like to take a brief moment to explain the two types of people that exercise in a weight room: the determined weight lifter and the common social lifter. The weight lifter is a dedicated person that utilizes his time wisely while working out. Every moment is spent either lifting a weight, doing a cardiovascular workout, or moving from one exercise to the next. However, a social lifter is one that will lift a weight here and there, maybe stop to take an extra rest, and talk to anyone in sight in order to pass the time. When they get home, they will say, "Honey, I worked out for two hours" when they really only exercised for about thirty minutes.

Dad, a social lifter, found that the fitness facility was actually quite nice. He decided to begin his grueling workout with some stretching, but when he looked into the mirror and noticed the amazing backside of a girl who was about twenty five years old and also stretching on the far side of the room, he just had to talk to her. As he slowly inched his way in the girl's direction, while simultaneously doing random exercises, he wondered who she was, and what he would ask her. Finally, after coming so close that he almost knocked her over while doing much too heavy pull-downs he said, "That is absolutely amazing! All I can say is once you've got it, don't let it go because it's hell trying to get it back."

The girl looking perplexed at first, finally said, "Oh, you mean your body."

"No, I mean your body," Dad said

"Well, I do try to stay in shape as much as possible," she said.

"Yeah, I used to be just like you, but as you can see I've been slacking off on the job for a couple of years," Dad said as he grabbed his belly.

"My name is Sylvia," she said as she held her hand out.

"Bob Koven, it's a pleasure to meet you. Did you say your last name was Corona? Dad asked with excitement.

"Yes, and to answer your next question, Dad is the CEO of the Corona Brewing Company. The big, three-hundred foot yacht anchored out in the bay is Dad's. I just came ashore to exercise and put my feet on firm ground," Sylvia said.

After learning all this, Dad was about to have a heart attack simply out of delight. "Yeah, I did notice that yacht out in the bay. I bet it takes quite a crew to handle that baby."

"Yes, it does. I kind of feel bad though because the crew has been working pretty hard lately. They're setting up for a big party that I am having tomorrow night," she said as she bent over to pick up a dumbbell. "Are you staying at the resort with anyone else?"

As Dad's eyes lit up he said, "Yes, I'm here with friends and my family for Spring Break. It was either here or the Four Seasons in Fiji, but my wife insisted on coming here."

"Well, if you would like, you and your guests may come to my party tomorrow evening. If your family and friends are as pleasant as you, it will be a splendid affair," Sylvia offered.

"Well, thank you very much. They will be delighted to learn of your invitation," Dad said as he placed a much too large amount of weight on the curling machine. The girl stayed in the fitness room for another twenty minutes and during the entire time, Dad attempted to lift more weight in more different ways than ever before. I believe that this was probably the best workout Dad ever had because afterwards he seemed to forget all of his earlier complaints about lack of exercise or the over-sized dinners.

The next day Dad asked Bobby if he would like to take a jet ski ride and look at the big yacht anchored outside the hotel. Bobby seemed uninterested, partly because he could think of a hundred things that could go wrong with Dad on a jet ski.

"What a beautiful day it is today. Bobby, wouldn't you agree?" Dad remarked with enthusiasm.

"Yes, it is a nice day. Why do you ask?" Bobby asked cautiously.

"Well, you know how you have been begging me to rent one of those jet skis on the beach?"

"Yes," Bobby said with growing suspicion.

"Well, I think today would be a perfect day get out on the water with one those things. I could even show you that big yacht out there," Dad said.

"Wait a minute. When I said I wanted to rent a jet ski, I meant that I would ride it alone. You know, because it might get a little awkward with you and me on it at the same time. Those things aren't exactly huge," Bobby said.

"It'll be fine. Just relax; what's wrong? You don't think I know how to handle one of those things? Don't you know I used to be a water-ski instructor back in high school?"

"Yes, but, Dad, these things don't have anything to do with water skiing. They're easy to turn over. All sorts of things could happen,"

"Jesus, Bobby, would you quit making excuses. You sound like an old fart. Come on!" Dad said as he left for the rental shack located on the beach.

After quickly filling out the paper work, they were off on a mid-size jet ski. Even though Dad had checked the "expert box" on the former waivers, he had never ridden a jet ski in his life and found it to be quite difficult. He started out driving while Bobby sat behind him holding on for his life. Anyone who has ridden as a passenger on a jet ski knows that it is not a very comfortable position. Soon, Bobby was becoming pretty tired of having to hold on, so he decided to switch positions. Dad agreed, and let Bobby take control of the watercraft.

"Now, Bobby you've seen how it's done. Just start out nice and easy," Dad said.

"I know how to drive, just hold on," Bobby said as he pressed the throttle down. After riding through random waves, Bobby decided to travel toward the massive yacht and look at its luxurious features. "Is it o.k. if we go over to the yacht and check it out?" Bobby asked.

"Of course, it is," Dad said happily. Now feeling as if he and his son were sharing some kind of ESP, he looked at the outside walkways and bow to see if the girl he met in the fitness center was there. "Just take it slow so you can admire the details," Dad said as he looked high and low. While cruising by on what was the fifth pass, he finally spotted Sylvia. She noticed Dad and began to wave, which caused Dad to forget about holding onto Bobby, and instead start to wave back.

"Hey, Mr. Koven!" shouted Sylvia.

"Hey, Sylvia! We were just admiring the yacht. It's unbelievable!" Dad shouted while waving. Meanwhile, Bobby noticed a perfect wave ahead that looked like an ample opportunity to catch at least three feet of air, and throttled toward it.

"Dad, look at that wave up there. Hold on!" Bobby said as he accelerated.

"What in the hell are you doing, Bobby! Slow down!" Dad screamed as he tried to find a place to hold onto.

"Just hold on!" repeated Bobby right before he steered the jet ski head first into the wave. I cannot imagine what Sylvia thought as she watched Dad, who is no small person by any means, do a back flip off the jet ski.

"You goddamn idio….." Dad screamed as his voice was drowned out by the incident.

Not only did this event leave Dad in a troubling and embarrassing situation, it left Bobby in an even worse predicament. Because of the weight imbalance caused by Dad suddenly leaving the back of the watercraft, the front end of the jet ski did a full nose dive and tossed Bobby into the water. Bobby did not only have to worry about getting his own ass back on the jet ski, he had to worry about getting Dad back onto the jet ski, which was an impossible task. Every time Bobby would get back onboard, Dad would pull him off trying to get himself onboard.

"You are an imbecile! I shouldn't have ever let you drive," Dad said as he floated in the water.

"Would you shut up and get back on the damn machine," Bobby said while trying to hold the jet ski steady.

"You get on first so you can help me up. O.K.!" Dad screamed.

"Alright, but I think it would be easier if you got on first," Bobby said

"I can't get on first, you asshole! You're gonna have to help me get on."

Once Bobby hoisted himself onboard, he held his hand out to Dad. "Take my hand," Bobby said.

As Dad grabbed Bobby's hand, he pulled with so much force that Bobby was dragged back into the water. "You have to put some muscle into, you pussy," Dad said as Bobby swam back over to the jet ski.

"If you weren't so fucking helpless, maybe I would," Bobby protested as he hoisted himself back onboard.

"Listen, you little bastard! If you don't quit back-talking me, I'm going to whip your ass!" Dad screamed from the water.

"Would you just be quiet and give me your hand," his son yelled.

"Did you tell me to calm down, goddamn it?" Dad said

"No, I said that I wanted you to be quiet. Jesus Christ! Just give me your hand."

After watching Bobby get dragged into the water for the fifth time and Dad going ballistic for about the tenth time, Sylvia said, "If you guys need some help, I can have a life raft pick you up."

"Thanks, but we don't need it," Dad shouted.

"That would be great, ma'am. You must excuse my father, he's delusional," Bobby shouted. Dad would have protested this comment, but by this time he was so tired from the relentless struggle that simply staying afloat required all of his remaining energy.

Soon after, a motorized raft approached Dad and Bobby. The men in the raft pulled Dad aboard and took him back to shore while Bobby rode the jet ski back to the rental shop, where he was charged for being over an hour late.

The invitation for the party on the yacht was never fulfilled due to the embarrassment and exhaustion that had overwhelmed Dad.

The Caribbean: Gilligan's Voyage

The next stop on the tour of wonderful travel memories is Nevis. An island located in the West Indies. Once again, the Keeters accompanied us on our Spring Break vacation that never seemed to be long enough. After we landed on the island of St. Kitts, we met some men from the resort where we would be staying. The men directed us to a shuttle that carried us to a dock where the resort's boat had been secured. It took the boat about forty five minutes to take us from St. Kitts to Nevis; however, it was during the journey between islands that I noticed something spectacular. The color of the water was unlike anything I had ever seen, and its transparency so lucid that the features of the ocean floor could be seen from the surface. So stunning was this sight that I had to make it known to Dad. When I turned toward him in order to get his attention he was busy speaking with the first mate. I should have expected that he would have already made friends with the first mate and embarked on an avid conversation. No matter where we travel, Dad always seems to be able to find a new friend or somebody who will engage in a conversation.

"Bob Koven" Dad said introducing himself to the first mate.

"Jasomi Malan," the first mate said as he shook hands with Dad.

"So, Jami, are you from Nevis or St. Kitts?" Dad asked as he made himself at home near the front of the boat.

"Well, I am from Nevis and I have lived here all my life," Jasomi replied.

"I bet growing up in a place like this must be bliss. Have you ever left the islands at all?"

"No sir, I have not. There is really no reason for me to leave this place. I can't imagine livin' anywhere else. Although, there is one thing that I have always wanted to see," Jasomi said.

"What's that?" Dad asked.

"I have always wanted to see and touch snow. I know that since you people are from America, you probably see it all the time, but I have never seen it," Jasomi said.

"By god, you're not missing much! There's not a snowflake's chance in hell that I would trade this weather for winter weather. Trust me, Jami, you've got the better deal." As Dad and Jasomi continued their conversation I knew it would be useless trying to divert my father's attention, so I found a seat near the side of the boat and enjoyed the scenery.

The island of Nevis was also one of the most beautiful natural land formations that had ever entered my life. As we approached the island, many details began to take distinct and vivid shapes. As my eyes followed the rolling waves of divine water toward the smooth sandy beach, I noticed tall slender palm trees that held bounties of coconuts near their tops. Behind the trees sat luxurious villas nestled between exotic flowers and plant life, and between the palm trees were lazy hammocks that vaporized any trace of stress lingering in the air.

Beyond the villas, dense jungle spread over the landscape like moss and a hovering cloud of mist sat around the higher elevations of jungle. There was also an inactive volcano poking through the jungle and jutting toward the clear blue sky. Because there was only one small town on the island and much of the island was not considered travel friendly, the resort on the island suggested that all guests stay within the resort's compound, which was rather large, and to Dad's dismay, it included a golf course.

When the boat came to a stop and was secured to the pier, we all stepped off and were greeted by a resort employee. The man directed us to the check-in counter where rooms were assigned. Finally, when we all reached our rooms we took a long nap. By the time everyone was rested and had organized all their belongings, it was time for dinner. As always, dinner included as many courses as possible in the longest feasible amount of time. As a child, two hours of continuous dining was beginning to really push the limit; moreover, as the three-hour mark would tick by, I truly though I was going to lose circulation in my legs due to the lack of movement. Bobby and I would always try to sit near each other so that we could talk leisurely throughout the marathon.

"Bobby," I whispered as we were getting ready to order.

"Yeah?"

"What do you think I should order? I really would like to try the lobster but the price says 'Market Value.' Don't you think it's probably really expensive?"

"Matt, first of all, we are on vacation in the Caribbean and second of all, if I am going to sit through a three hour to four hour dinner, then I think that the lobster would be deserving of my time spent here," Bobby replied.

"That's a good point. Besides, with all the drinks and everything else that Mom, Dad, and the Keeters order, there's a good chance that they wouldn't even notice," I said with enthusiasm.

Three and a half hours later I stood up for the first time since dinner began and felt as if I weighed a metric ton. I knew that if I was feeling this bad, Dad had to have be feeling ten times worse. Once back in his room, he said, "Here we go again on this goddamn eat till you can't see diet. I like vacations, but I don't like eating and grazing the entire vacation," he complained.

"Well, maybe you can sleep late in the morning and just relax. If you sleep late enough, you can skip breakfast and just eat lunch," Mom suggested.

"That would sound great if I was actually on a vacation, but I'm not because I've got to play golf every goddamn day of the week! I can't imagine what it would be like to actually spend a day on the beach or the water. God forbid that Jim doesn't play a round of golf for a day. Besides, you know how damm hot it is up in that jungle with all of those damn chimpanzees. It's ridiculous," Dad grumbled.

"Well, Jim knows you sent the boys to that sailing camp over the summer. Maybe you can tell him that you want to go out on the water with them for a day instead of playing golf."

"Yeah that sounds like a good idea. I think I'll sleep on it," Dad said as he lay down for the night.

The next day Dad played a round of golf with Jim, while Mom, Julie, Kaylan, Bobby, and I spent the day on the beach. During the day, Mom, Bobby, and I took the opportunity to rent a sailboat for Dad and ourselves.

The previous summer, my parents had sent Bobby and me to a sailing camp in order to learn the sport. We both thoroughly enjoyed the experience even though it really just served as a day care to watch us while my parents took a vacation. However, in order to show Dad how much we had learned, as if our skills had to have the grand approval by the great man himself, and to give him a golf break, we rented the small catamaran for two hours.

"Are you sure you guys can handle this sailboat?" Mom asked.

"Mom, there's nothing to worry about. Bobby and I were the expert sailors at camp," I exclaimed with confidence.

"O.k.. It's just that you know how he can get if something goes wrong," Mom warned as she signed the waiver for the boat.

The next day, Dad was able to escape his terrors of golf by explaining the sailing situation to Jim at breakfast.

"Listen, Jim, I think I'm going to have to skip out on golf for today. I promised the boys I would go sailing with them to see what they learned at that camp Gale and I sent them to last summer," Dad said.

"No problem, Bob. I was thinking about getting out on the beach myself. It's so beautiful," Jim remarked.

"Yeah it truly is. But listen, they didn't rent the boat until about three o' clock. I'd be happy to play cards on the beach and relax until then," Dad offered.

"Sounds good. You'll probably need some relaxing anyway before you get out on that boat," Jim joked.

"Yeah, you're probably right," Dad said.

As three o'clock approached Dad left his card game and went to tell Mom that he was headed to the rental shack to get the boat.

"Where's Bobby and Matt?" Dad asked.

"They're already waiting on you at the rental shack. Do you want some sun tan lotion; the sun is pretty intense," Mom said.

"Hell, no! I hate that sticky stuff. Besides, we'll only be gone for about forty-five minutes," Dad said.

"You know you have sensitive skin," Mom responded.

"Gale, I'm not a goddamn sissy," Dad protested as he walked toward the rental shack. When he arrived, Bobby and I had already pushed the catamaran into the water. "You guys ready?" our smiling Dad asked.

"We're ready if you're ready," Bobby answered.

"O.k.. Let's go," Dad said as he sat down on the side of the catamaran.

Once we were all onboard, I skippered, and we headed north along the coast. The wind was good and we steadily picked up speed while on a close haul tack. As we approached the port of Jamestown, the only town on the island, boat traffic started to become much busier. There were barges, yachts, and many other types of boats traveling in every direction. As we sailed along, I noticed a barge approaching from the starboard side. Of course, being the ignorant fool that I was, I believed that our 4x4 vessel had the right of way, and that the immense barge had to yield for us. While we inched along, the barge continued to advance toward us. Finally, when the barge was beginning to look like an approaching mountain about to run us over, Dad shouted, "What in the hell are you doing!"

"Dad, just calm down. We have the right of way," I explained.

"Does that barge look like it gives a shit what your right of way is?" Dad screamed.

I did not answer, but quickly tacked into the opposite direction, which turned us toward the open sea. In order to calm Dad down and get us out of harm's way, I decided that I would steer far enough away from the port so that we would not be in danger of other boats or Dad's displeasure. When we had traveled to the point where the coastline looked like a thick line above the water, the wind completely stopped. Even the waves had diminished to small ripples that drifted effortlessly past us.

"Bobby I think I would feel much better if you took control," Dad said.

"Dad, it doesn't matter who is skippering because there is no wind," I objected.

"There's always goddamn wind. You just have to be able to find it. Now let your brother take control," Dad retorted.

"Fine!" I said as Bobby and I switched places.

After Bobby assumed his position at the rudder, I sat baking alongside Dad in the miserable baking heat. The unrelenting sun was directly above us, which did not allow the sail to lend any shadow. While Bobby was desperately trying to find the smallest trace of wind to harness, Dad and I grew more and more uncomfortable in the smoldering heat.

Finally, after about twenty minutes had passed, Dad said, "Jesus Christ! I feel like a goddamn hot tamale. Bobby, what in the hell did I send you guys to that sailing camp for? You both are the poorest excuse for sailors that I have ever seen."

Bobby tried to reason. "If there was some damn wind, I could sail. Look at the water. It's completely flat."

I nodded. "Bobby is right. I mean, there's literally no wind, and without wind we're not going to be going anywhere."

"We better be going somewhere because if you guys think I'm going to spend the goddamn day roasting my ass off on this fucking excuse for a sailboat, you guys are wrong. I'll swim to the fucking shore before I spend the night out here," our father said.

"You know, there are barracudas in these waters," I said.

"All I know is that you guys couldn't sail a fucking banana peel across a toilet bowl if your lives depended upon it," Dad yelled.

"Just calm down," Bobby said.

"I'm not going to calm down, goddamn it!" Dad screamed.

"If you don't calm down, we'll never make it back," Bobby's voice sounded threatening.

"If you tell me to calm down one more time, you're never going to make it back because I'm going to throw your ass in the water!"

The three of us argued for at least another hour until a slight breeze began to blow across the water. However, it was too late because by this time Dad resembled a red pepper. Slowly but surely we made our way back to the resort. Four and a half hours later, we finally set foot on land.

"I have been worried sick!" Mom said as she watched us hobble across the beach toward her.

"If you ever send me on a goddamn eight-hour tour with those crazy fucks again, I think I'll drown myself," Dad said, sounding quite upset.

"You look like hell," Mom said.

"I'm dehydrated, burned to a fucking crisp, and can barely walk. It's a wonder I didn't have a fucking stroke," Dad said.

"Let's just get you back to the room. I was about to send a rescue crew after you guys," Mom said.

"You should have sent them the minute we left," Dad replied as he slowly made his way to the room.

"I didn't think he was ever going to shut up," I said to Bobby and we walked toward our room.

"Yeah well, we did kinda screw up," my brother said.

The next day Dad's sunburn was unmistakably bad. Just the sight of his cherry red skin made me cringe. Although Bobby and I had a slight burn from our exposure, we had also taken Mom's advice and used plenty of sunscreen before we went on our boating adventure. While the Keeters, Bobby, Mom, and I spent the remainder of our vacation enjoying snorkeling, swimming, and suntanning, Dad spent much of the time recovering while reading books on the finer points of sailing.

4

Next Stop, Spain!

Weeks before we left for our vacation to Spain, Dad continually asked, "Is everyone preparing for Spain? Everyone needs...." However, I think that the proper question to have been asking was, "Is Spain ready for us?" I already knew that traveling to a foreign country where the language is different with an extremely dysfunctional American family would create some problems.

Spain: Navigation 101

Although this spring break vacation in Spain was going to be without our friends, the Keeters, we were not going to be completely alone because my grandparents had already traveled to Madrid and we were planning to meet them there. Since this trip involved a lot of traveling by plane and train, the day before we left, Dad bought those neat travel bags that are usually black, roll on wheels, and fit easily in an overhead compartment.

"Yep, no more waiting for our bags at the baggage claim," Dad said when he came home with the new luggage.

"These look wonderful," Mom said as she examined the black bags.

"They're the top of the line, too. You won't believe the deal that I got on them! The man at the store gave me a great price. He said they're a little wider than most, but that all planes and trains have big enough overhead compartments to hold them," Dad said proudly.

The next day, as we headed for the airport, I began having that familiar feeling: something crazy and confusing was going to happen soon. This feeling was confirmed when we boarded the plane with our new luggage and began to stow them in the overhead compartment. One of the four bags slid in smoothly. The other three were about a quarter of an inch too wide.

"This goddamn thing!" Dad muttered as he attempted to slam his bag against the compartment opening while blocking the aisle for other passengers. After about the ninth attempt, Dad said, "Bobby, try and put my bag in the compartment. I'm worn out."

While Bobby now attempted to do the same with the luggage, the ensuing commotion attracted the attention of a stewardess who approached Dad and said, "Sir, if you or your son cannot fit your luggage in the overhead compartment, it will have to be stored in the cargo section of the airplane."

"I'm not storing my luggage in the cargo section of the plane. I brought these bags so that I could specifically use them as carry-on luggage," Dad said as Bobby continued to try and jam the bags into the compartment.

"Sir, I'm sorry but your luggage doesn't seem to fit or meet the carry on luggage requirements. If you would," the stewardess was saying as Dad interrupted.

"Lady, I'm sure there must be room somewhere in the cabin for my luggage so if you wouldn't mind stepping out of the way," Dad said as he directed his attention toward Bobby and me and said, "You guys take the three bags that won't fit and find another place where they will fit."

As we headed down the aisle past the stewardess, she called out, "Wait a minute! You guys cannot just put your luggage anywhere you want. It must be stored below!"

"Madam, both my boys have been diagnosed with chronic asthma. We keep all their medicine in our luggage and keep our luggage with us so that if one of them has an attack, we will have the medicine handy," Dad lied.

"Well, I am sorry. I didn't have any idea that this was the case," apologized the stewardess.

"Well, it is the case," Dad said as he looked beyond the stewardess to view Bobby and me successfully finding a place in the first-class section of the plane to store the luggage. As I sat down in my seat, I wondered if there had ever been a trip where Dad had not pissed somebody off within the first thirty minutes. I concluded that there had not been such a time, and I began to fall asleep in order to pass the next twelve hours as quickly as possible.

We arrived in Madrid around two o' clock a.m. The airport was not terribly busy so we were able to quickly find our rental car, and because we did not have to wait at the baggage claim we did not lose any time. Once having loaded all the luggage into the station wagon, our first objective was to travel to my grandparents' hotel, which no one knew how to find. Equipped with a map and a psychotic driver we were off on what would be a ride to remember. Although the map had easy to read street names, the names of the streets were not on signs, but on the sides of buildings. This minor detail posed quite a problem.

"Your mother said that we needed to take a left on Hidalgo Street," Dad said to Mom as we pulled out of the airport.

"Yes, the map says that it should be up here just a little ways," Mom said squinting at the map of Madrid.

"That's funny I can't seem to find the names of any of the streets. Matt, can you find any?" Dad asked.

"I don't see any names either," I replied.

"Well, this is ridiculous. We'll be driving all day if we can't find the names of the streets," Dad said as we continued to cruise along the road. Soon, the road began to branch into smaller ones and Dad took random routes.

When we took the fifth random road, Bobby said, "I think the names of the road are printed on the sides of the buildings."

As Mom began to search for the street name that we had most recently past she said, "Bob, I can't seem to find where we are on the map."

"My God! We're as lost as last year's Easter egg. Give the map to Bobby and see if he can find where we are," Dad instructed. "Can you find where we are?" Dad asked after about thirty seconds.

"If you would give me a minute, I might be able to," Bobby replied irritated.

"If I give you a minute, we'll be completely lost," Dad said.

"We already are completely lost. Besides, I can't seem to find where we are either," Bobby said.

"That's just great. Now we're lost in Madrid. I don't having a fucking clue as to where I am going. I'm just driving. If it wasn't for you nitwits reading the map, we wouldn't be lost." Dad's tone was livid as he began to accelerate down a narrow street out of anger.

At about the point when I could barely see pedestrians, Dad spotted two women whom he thought, for some reason, would give us directions. He ripped the steering wheel to the right, causing the station wagon to skid onto a gravel parking lot. Once off the street, he pulled a hard left while mashing down on the brake pedal, and we came to a fishtailing stop next to the two women, who happened to be from London. Even if the women had known where the hotel was, I do not think that they would have told us, primarily because they were now sprayed with dirt and gravel, and secondly, because of Dad's demanding voice.

"Do you ladies happen to know where the Palacio Real Hotel is located or how to get there?" Dad demanded.

As one of the women turned to the other one, she said, "Now, Mary, is that not the pleasant little hotel we saw last week while shopping for that splendid tea pot?"

"I don't know, Elizabeth. It's just that we have," the other started to say when Dad interrupted them.

"Gale, these women are useless!" Dad exclaimed as he slammed the gear shift into drive and floored the gas pedal, causing even more dirt and gravel to rise into the air. We hit the street at a perpendicular angle with tires squealing, and as we caught air while ramping the median, I noticed an oncoming palm tree on the upcoming sidewalk. We plowed into the palm tree soon enough, causing Dad to shift into reverse, but he hit the gear with such force that the knob came away in his hand.

"This goddamn rice rocket," he yelled as he threw the knob out of the window. "I hate Spain, I hate Madrid, I hate everything about this goddamn place," he yelled as he proceeded to engage in an amazing 180-degree turn, grab what was left of the gear shift, and threw it into drive. As we left the chaotic scene, there was nothing but smoke, gravel, dust, and the two British women standing near the road. I could not help but wonder what they must have been thinking as they witnessed the confusion. Now, no one knew exactly where we were headed until we noticed that the cars in front of us were headed straight toward us! We had been traveling the wrong way on a one-way road!

Although everyone in the car had been in too much shock to say anything, when I noticed the oncoming cars, I felt it was an appropriate time to scream, "Look out!" as I pointed in front of us.

Dad quickly swerved off the street and turned around before the oncoming traffic caught us. Even though we averted a collision, many of the drivers felt it necessary to protest our antics. As multiple horns honked, Dad screamed, "Fuck you, you Spanish sons of bitches!" while flipping the bird. Dad was a superb multi task person.

Once we were headed with the flow of traffic Mom said, "Bob I think you should pull into a gas station and ask for directions."

"Fine! I'm done driving. You can get the directions and drive us to the hotel because I can't take it any longer," Dad said as he pulled into a gas station.

"Obviously," Bobby remarked while quickly getting out of the car knowing what his comment would invoke. Inside the gas station

Bobby helped Mom ask for directions in Spanish, and when they got back into the car, Mom switched places with Dad and drove the rest of the way to the hotel. We didn't get lost once.

When we finally reached my grandparents' hotel, everyone was relieved.

"What a ride from hell," Dad said as we stepped out of the station wagon.

"Yeah really," Mom said.

As we walked toward the entrance, I noticed two people on a balcony about thirty stories up who looked kind of like my grandparents.

"Look!" I said to Dad. "I think that's grandma and grandpa, and pointed in their direction.

Quickly cupping his hands over his mouth, Dad shouted "Hey, Sue, you know what in the hell we went through trying to find this damn place!" The elderly woman began to wave. "I hope you guys haven't emptied the liquor out of this place yet because I'm sure as hell going to need a drink," Dad continued. He started to say something else; when I noticed my real grandparents walk out onto a balcony that was on the second floor. "Dad, I made a mistake. Sorry, but grandma and grandpa are right there," I pointed toward the second floor and began laughing.

"That's just typical," Dad said after he stopped shouting up to the wrong people. We finally went into the hotel, and everyone including Bobby and me, had a drink.

Spain: The Pharmacia

As one can imagine, it is easy to get sick in a foreign country when you are exposed to environments, food and water that you are not used to. While in Spain, I caught a cold that was making my vacation miserable.

It was a hot Sunday afternoon and we had just left the Prado Museum in Madrid. We were on our way back to our hotel in a taxi. "I feel horrible," I said.

"What's wrong?" Mom asked.

"I'll tell you what's wrong. He ate too much of that chocolate for breakfast this morning at the hotel," Dad interjected.

"That is not what's wrong." I said while resting my head against the taxi window. "I feel like hell, I can't breath through my nose, my eyes are watery, and I'm burning up,"

"Well, how do you expect me to fix it?" whined Dad from the front seat. We're in goddamn Spain. All of the medicine is written in Spanish."

"Oh, Bob! I'm sure you can find something," Mom said, annoyed.

Dad looked around for a while and suddenly asked, "Bobby, how do say pharmacy in Spanish?"

"A 'pharmacia' is a pharmacy in Spanish," replied Bobby as he rolled his eyes.

The taxicab driver, Ricardo, was silent during the entire conversation until Dad said, "Ricardo, necessita un pharmacia for mi son," as he pointed toward me.

Ricardo looked confused at first, but after Dad repeated the phrase numerous times, Ricardo said, "O si, si senor. Pero las farmacias son cerradas el domingo. Sin embargo, pienso que sé dónde uno pudo estar abierto."

"Bobby, what in Jesus' name did he say?" Dad asked.

"He said that all the pharmacies are closed on Sundays, but he might know where one is open," Bobby said with a bored look.

Dad signaled Ricardo an o.k. sign with his hand and we began our search for an open pharmacy. I watched the electronic meter continue to rise as the minutes ticked by. Finally, we came to a three-way intersection with a pharmacy located in between two streets that joined at the intersection. Ricardo quickly parallel parked, pointed to the pharmacy, and said, "Allí es."

Dad peered at the building with narrowed eyes and said, "I think that's the one. I'll be back in less than fifteen minutes. Stay here." We all watched as he stepped out of the car and made his way across the busy intersection. He entered the busy pharmacy and found that the situation was worse than he had predicted. There were thousands of different colored and labeled drugs stacked everywhere, written in various Spanish dialects. "Mmmm.... let's see," Dad said as he made his way to the counter.

A pharmacist from behind the counter quickly approached Dad. "¿Hay algo que puedo ayudarle con el, Señor?"

"Uhhh, well, I necessita some medicina for mi son. He tener ache in his cabeza y he no," Dad was saying as the pharmacist interrupted.

"I'm sorry, you are American," said the pharmacist.

"You can speak English! Thank God!" rejoiced Dad. "My family and I are spending about ten days in Spain and my youngest son has gotten sick. I need something for headaches, fever, and congestion," Dad said almost happily.

"I think I have exactly what you need," the pharmacist said as he walked to an aisle and picked up an orange striped box. "This is a powder, so all you have to do is pour it in a drink or on food and let him eat it. He should feel better in a day or so." The pharmacist handed the box to Dad.

"Are there any side effects?" Dad asked with concern.

"None that I know of," the pharmacist replied as Dad paid for the medicine. Although it had taken twenty minutes, Dad had successfully purchased the correct type of medicine in a Spanish pharmacy. Everyone would assume that Dad had effectively communicated with a Spanish pharmacist, and Dad would be sure to gloat about his accomplishment when he reached the car. However, reaching the car proved to be more challenging than buying the medicine.

Waiting for Dad in the miserable heat was not much fun. Ricardo did not say a word, and all I could think about was Dad bringing me some medicine. During twenty minutes of waiting, I noticed that most of the cars parked along the street were the same color and looked the same. I thought how boring it would be to live in a place where most of the cars are the same model and color. Then my attention caught the rising meter in the front of the taxi, and as I watched the numbers flash, I saw Dad coming out of the pharmacy with a smile on his face.

"There's your father," Mom said as we all shifted our focus toward him. Dad walked to the street corner, waited for a clearing in traffic, and quickly ran across the street. Next, he began to make his way in our direction, passing other parked cars. When he was about four cars away from us, Dad suddenly stopped and reached for the handle of a parked car that looked strikingly like ours. It looked exactly like the one that we were in, but it was a privately owned car and the owner was sleeping inside it. Dad was on the passenger's side of the vehicle, resulting in his obstruction of oncoming traffic.

The door handle was locked, and as Dad began to repeatedly yank on it he began to yell, "Open the goddamn door!" as cars buzzed by within inches of him, honking, loudly and angrily.

"Oh my god! What is he doing?" Mom screamed.

"I have no idea," Bobby said with astonishment. Ricardo began to honk in order to get Dad's attention, but the honking blended in with all the other honking that was going on. As we sat helplessly and watched Dad simultaneously flick people off and try for the door handle, we could not help but laugh. Even Ricardo was laughing.

"Open the goddamn door you, nitwits! What are you guys trying to do? Get me killed?!" Dad hollered at the top of his lungs.

"HHHHOOOONNNNKKKK!!!!"

"Hey, fuck you, you Spanish sonofabitch. Yeah see what happens when you run over my ass!" Dad shouted as he pressed himself up against the car in order to avoid becoming road kill. The "wrong" car rocked so hard when Dad pressed himself up against it, and the man sleeping inside of the car woke up.

"My God! The man sleeping inside the car just woke up," Bobby said

"Oh no, we should help him," Mom said. But before Mom could get out of the car, the man being harassed by Dad noticed that someone was trying to get into his car. The man panicked and jumped to the opposite side of the car while fumbling to find his keys. Once having found his keys, he jumped back into the driver's seat, started the car, and tore out of the parking place. Dad was almost run over, and as he watched the car speed away, he threw his arms up in the air and said, "What in the fuck was that all about? Those assholes!"

"Bob! Over here, you idiot!" shouted Mom. She walked toward him.

"What?" Dad said with confusion and embarrassment.

"What was wrong with telling me I had the wrong car?" Dad asked.

"Nothing. It was just so funny," Mom said laughing as she made her way with Dad back to the taxi.

When he stepped into the taxi, Ricardo laughed and patted him on the back. Not saying a word, Dad handed me the medicine and ordered Ricardo to take us to our hotel. After Dad had "survived" the streets of Madrid, I think he was so happy to be back at the hotel to rest, he didn't even complain about how expensive the cab ride was.

Spain: Universal Language

Throughout the entire trip, Dad had been raving on and on about tapas, appetizers that many restaurants in Spain serve in the evening before dinner. In all our previous nights in Spain, we had always arrived at a restaurant too late to eat tapas, so we made ourselves a promise to finally get to a restaurant early enough to eat tapas.

"What time is it, Gale?" Dad asked as we were walking back to our hotel from an afternoon of shopping in Seville.

"It's fifteen past five. Why do you ask?" replied Mom merrily swinging her shopping bags back and forth.

"Well, I've been wanting you guys to try some tapas, but we always eat dinner too late. If we hurry, we just might be able to make it in time," Dad said enthusiastically.

"Maybe we could eat tapas tomorrow night," Mom said. "We'd just be in such a rush trying to get to the restaurant tonight that it wouldn't be enjoyable."

"It won't be that much of a rush," Dad persisted. "Besides, this is our last day in Seville, and I read about a famous tapas restaurant here that is supposed to be out of this world."

Mom was still reluctant, but said "Well, if you insist."

"Then, we can go see some flamenco dancing," Dad said with a smile.

"That would be wonderful!" Mom said, this time with great enthusiasm. Bobby and I followed behind our parents, listening to our evening plans as we approached the hotel.

Of course, everyone had to take a shower and change clothes before we went to eat tapas. Although one would think everyone would feel better and more relaxed after getting ready, it always turned out to be the complete opposite. Dad yells at everyone to hurry up and get dressed, then he is always the last to be ready. Even with a separate room for Bobby and me, it was a very stressful situation for everyone.

"Let's go, goddamn it! We gotta be outta here in fifteen minutes!" Dad shouted, still in his underwear while watching TV.

"Everyone is ready except you," shouted Bobby through the wall that divided the two hotel rooms.

"Gale! Are you about done in there?" Dad yelled toward the bathroom where a hairdryer had been blowing for twenty minutes.

"Almost, honey!" Mom shouted back.

"Well, could you please hurry it up? I've gotta sit down before my ass explodes. You know I've been stoved up all day."

"Sit down where?" she asked.

"On the goddamn toilet! Where else?" Dad screamed.

"Sorry! It's your fault that you've got to go so bad. You ate all of that greasy pork for lunch, and then you devoured that entire bucket of oiled olives," Mom said as she finally turned off the hair dryer.

"Are you done yet?" Dad asked.

"Yes, I am done, but you better hurry up. Especially if you're going to sit down," Mom said.

"Don't start. The last thing I need is someone telling me how fast I have to take a shit and get dressed," Dad responded.

Bobby and I sat in our room, listening and watching TV, and as we heard the "thunk" of the toilet seat, Bobby rolled his eyes and said, "Jesus! Now it's going to be another twenty minutes."

"Yep. I think we're going to miss tapas time once again," I said.

As usual, we left the hotel in our beat-up station wagon fifteen minutes late, and drove straight into a traffic jam. By the time we made it to the restaurant, they had finished serving tapas and had moved on to serving dinner.

We entered the restaurant and approached the host. "Señor, esteis sirviendo tapas?" Bobby asked.

"No, estamos sirviendo cena," he replied.

Bobby turned to Dad and said, "He says they've stopped serving tapas and are now serving dinner."

"What do you mean?" Dad asked as he moved his eyes toward the host. "Tell this idiot that we came all the way from America to eat his goddamn tapas. This is ridiculous."

"Do you want to go somewhere else?" Mom asked.

"No, damn it. Let's just eat here. We have to be at the flamenco place in two hours anyway," Dad said. He signaled the host to seat us. We were taken to the only available table, which was located outside near the street in a corner. The table was not just outside near the street, it was literally inches from the curb.

"Is this the only table that you have available?" Dad asked the host.

Looking a little confused at first, the host finally said, "Si, si."

"O.k. then," Dad said. Everyone took a seat. When the host left, Dad asked, "Did he give us any menus?"

"No," Mom answered.

"Matt, signal the next waiter you see and get him to bring us some menus," Dad ordered. After we all became a little more comfortable, we began to talk about the past few days and what was to come.

"Well, I have had a wonderful time in Spain so far," Mom said energetically. "And Bob, once you learned how to drive, it hasn't been so bad getting around."

"I apologize for my crazy driving in Madrid. It was unacceptable," Dad said seriously.

"I just want to know what those two English ladies were thinking when after getting sprayed with dirt and gravel, they watched us smash into that palm tree," I said with a laugh.

"I guess it was kind of funny," Dad said grinning and leaning back in his chair. However, as Dad leaned back he positioned himself precariously close to the busy narrow street.

Cars were passing within inches of him. "HHHOOOOONNNN-KKKK!!"

The noise made everyone jump. "Jesus Christ! I'm in the middle of fucking traffic," Dad cried out as he scooted his chair closer to the table. By the time we had moved onto something else to discuss, everyone could see that the cars that were passing within inches of Dad's chair were beginning to really annoy him. Moreover, it was about this time that he realized it had been thirty minutes since we had been seated, and we had not even been given menus.

"Matt! Have you not found a fucking waiter yet?" Dad protested.

"I've been trying to get one's attention, but they just walk by," I said.

"What in the hell is going on? First, they stick us over herr in the corner in the middle of fucking traffic, they don't give us menus, and they don't even wait on us!" Dad griped as the rest of us grew quiet. "By God, the next one of those Spanish bastards that passes by here without stopping is going to get it." Finally, one of the waiters walked by and began to drift farther away and Dad screamed, "Hey, Fuckhead!!" I have never heard such an abrupt silence in my life. Even though Dad's comment was in English, everyone, including the people inside the restaurant, turned around and looked at us.

"Bob!" Mom uttered softly.

During the horrible silence, the waiter looked at Dad and pointed to himself as if asking, "Who me?" Dad pointed his finger at the waiter with such intensity that it looked as if he had shot the man.

With everyone in the restaurant now watching, the waiter walked wearily to our table and with a Castilian accent said, "Is there a problem sir?"

"Hell, yes, there's a problem, goddamn it, you English speaking bastard!" Dad shouted as a manager came toward our table to listen. "Since we arrived over thirty minutes ago, we have not received menus or been given a waiter. Not to mention the fact that, you guys seated us at possibly the worst table in this whole goddamn place!"

The manager gave the waiter standing nearby a disappointed look and then said to Dad, "Sir, I hope you will accept my apologies for the inconvenience that you have encountered." The manager then motioned for some menus. "If you are not already inclined to leave, I will have someone take your order immediately and you shall have your meal as fast as possible, free of charge, if you will not make another scene," the manager said quietly.

"Since you are confident that our meals will be served shortly, we will stay, but only because I have heard this is a good restaurant," Dad said.

"Thank you, sir," the manager replied. He walked away quickly and gestured to another waiter.

Even though I wanted to crawl under the table the entire time, our food was on the table within ten minutes and the meal was great. The food was served so fast that we were able to make it to the flamenco parlor on time. To this day, I still wonder whether it was the actual words that caused all the people in the restaurant to stop, or if it was simply Bob Koven's shouting.

5

Bailing Your Kids Out 101

Although kids around the globe are scolded for misbehaving and getting into trouble, I believe that for the most part, Dads actually enjoy hearing that their kid has misbehaved from time to time. I'm not saying that it is good for kids to be misbehaving all the time, just occasionally to prove that they are still human. It's a realistic conjecture that after scolding their kid for acting up, a "normal" Dad will be on the phone with his best friend laughing about what his kid achieved. However, as I have learned, the funniest situations are the ones that are the least funny when they happen, because if they are funny to you, Dad may not step in and bail you out of whatever predicament you got yourself into.

The 11-Year-Old Terrorist

An airport can be a scary place for a nine and eleven-year-old. This was exactly what Mom was thinking when she bought Bobby a can of pepper spray for self-protection when sending her sons on a trip across the country to visit our grandparents in Iowa. I'm not positive, but I can imagine that the whole idea of sending us away by ourselves was Dad's idea. Nevertheless, Bobby and I made the trip safely to Iowa, where we spent the days looking at the endless cornfields and wondering how in the world anyone could live there. Although I love my grandparents dearly, by the time you leave their house after any amount of time, you feel as if you need a new pair of lungs thanks to the excess of second-hand smoke. This fact, coupled with plain old homesickness and we were ready to leave Iowa, however, we had one last stop to make. On the way home, we were to stop in St. Louis to visit my Aunt Connie, Uncle Max, Cousin Max, Cousin Julie, and Cousin Kathy. We spent one night there enjoying the abundance of junk food, which we are not used to because at home someone was always in the dieting stage that never seemed to work. But, when you stayed at Aunt Connie's house, junk food was forced upon you. Connie had one of those dieting mentalities that fed on another person's failure to eat healthy. Once we had our fill of our kind kinfolk, Connie happily drove us to the airport. After buying us a mass of St. Louis key chains, hats, and other junk, we were off headed home. As we were boarding the plane, I noticed Bobby was playing with the pepper spray canister in his pocket.

"Would you quit messing with that thing. It makes me nervous," I said as I walked through the entrance of the plane.

"Gosh, you're such a baby. It's not like I'm going to spray it in your eyes," Bobby said.

"Just put it away," I said. Not thinking much more about it, I continued to board the plane and find my seat. An older man in an aisle seat did not look too happy when he discovered that Bobby and I would be sitting next to him. As we settled in, Bobby continued to play with the pepper spray bottle between his legs. Finally, when the plane was in the midst of taking off, Bobby accidentally pressed the spray button on the bottle. As I watched him do this, the spray passed within a foot of my face. Startled, I waited for the burning of the eyes to begin; however, it did not and instead, Bobby and I were left looking at each other. Bobby quickly asked, "Did the pepper spray just go off?"

"Yes, you moron," I replied.

"No it didn't," Bobby denied.

"Yes, it did, and it was within inches of my face. You better be glad that it didn't get in my eyes, you idiot," I said angrily.

"You're hallucinating, nothing happened," he said and nervously slipped the small bottle into his pocket. Just then the elderly man sitting next to us began to cough uncontrollably. I quickly looked at

Bobby and motioned to the man coughing next to me. "He has a cold," Bobby said, reassuringly.

"Yeah right," I said, sarcastically. Apparently, when pepper spray is inhaled, it quickly begins to burn the lungs and causes coughing. I wish the man's coughing had been a simple cold, but when all the plane's passengers started making choking sounds and coughing loudly, I knew it was not a cold. The captain was coughing into his radio, the flight attendant explaining how to wear a seat belt lost her voice, and then I began to cough.

"Huuuooww. Huuuooowwaaahahah!" the captain coughed over the speaker and radio system. "Ladies and gentleman, huuuoooww-waah, excuse me, but there seems to be a problem with the circulation or the, huuuoooowwwwaahaha. My god, there is definitely something wrong with the air. We will be, huuwoowwwahaa, making an emergency landing. Please stay calm and do not panic. Thank you," the captain choked as the oxygen masks located above everyone's head dropped out of the ceiling.

We landed within the next ten minutes. Before landing, a flight attendant tried to explain the procedure while simultaneously choking to death.

"Alright, hhuhwoohahaha, when we land, the emergency exits must be opened. Inflattable slides will inflate and everyone must exit in an orderly fashion," she said.

Once we landed, the emergency doors were quickly opened and everyone on the plane stampeded for the nearest exit. While passengers were getting off the plane, men in plastic suits with oxygen tanks were running toward the plane. The men had large vacuums and once onboard, they began to suck up the hazardous air. While Bobby and I walked innocently off the plane, still coughing, there was a man with an earpiece standing on a bench giving directions to the frightened travelers.

"Look what you did, you fool," I said quietly to Bobby while we walked away from the plane.

"How was I supposed to know a little squirt was going to fuck up the entire plane?" he retorted.

We noticed that the old man who had been sitting next to us now looked at us and then proceeded to walk to the man on the bench and point in our direction. I knew we were goners.

"Look!" I said to Bobby as I pointed to the old man. "That man is going to tell on us."

"Damn," Bobby said. He walked to the man who was still trying to calm the passengers and handed him the bottle of pepper spray as the old man stood by. Bobby said, "I found this on the airplane while we were evacuating."

"He didn't find that on the plane," the old man exclaimed. "He and the little one were talking about that stuff the whole time. It about killed me!"

The man standing on the bench looked suspiciously at Bobby and immediately radioed for assistance. Soon after, a man dressed in black, who looked like the Hulk himself, approached us. He looked down at my brother and me and said, "I'll be traveling with you on your journey to Atlanta. There better not be any misbehaving this time." Neither of us replied; we just looked at each other and walked with the man to a second plane that would serve as our transportation home.

The flight seemed abnormally long and quiet. It was a relief to finally land and see Dad waiting to pick us up at the terminal. Already mad that the plane was late, Dad watched as every passenger came into the waiting area and after what seemed to be the last person, he began to wonder if we were even on the plane.

"How in the hell did they miss the flight? I bet Connie got to the airport late," he said to himself.

However, we finally did appear, each of us accompanied by one arm of the amazing Hulk, who sternly looked at Dad and said, "Mr. Koven, there has been a major problem concerning your two sons, and you must come with me."

Dad looked like a raging bull that had been caught off guard. He quickly shot that horrible look of his at both of us, and with the most intense words ever, he said, "What in the blazes of hell did you two do!!"

There was no comment of course; we all just followed the monster in black down several stairscases until we came to the basement of Hartsfield International Airport. There were hallways of rooms, and the man in black finally stopped at one and led us inside. It looked like an interrogation room and reminded me of the ones that detectives use on TV crime shows. We all had a seat at the single table located in the center of the chamber.

"First, I want a phone so that I can call my lawyer," Dad said immediately.

"No problem, follow me," the Hulk said pointing to the phone on the wall.

While on the phone, two more men came and sat down in front of us. After another minute, Dad hung up the phone and sat down on our side of the table.

"My name is Bob Jamison and this is my partner, Jack Friar," the larger of the two men said as he motioned toward the other one. "We are here to try and figure out what, why, and how this disaster took place," he said.

"I have no idea what my two sons have done," Dad said, glaring at us. "So if someone would care to explain, I would appreciate it."

Bobby and the larger man began to both explain what happened and when the larger man said the words "pepper spray," Dad's eyes filled with surprise.

"Where in the hell did you get pepper spray?"

"Mom bought it for me," Bobby said, his voice wavering.

"Mom bought it for you!" Dad repeated. "Why did Mom buy it for you?"

"She was worried about our safety," Bobby explained.

"Jesus Christ! Nobody ever tells me anything!" Dad exclaimed as he grabbed his forehead. I thought he was going to die right then and there, but he just turned away and said, "Can I call my lawyer again?" After hours of having to talk to officials from the FAA, FBI, and various other organizations, the men finally released us and told us that they would be in contact soon.

As we later remembered, the man who was questioning Bobby was named Bob. As a result, one day we received a phone call from an FBI official in Washington that was asking Dad, also named Bob, "What should we do with the pepper spray kids in Atlanta?"

"I think we should forget about it and focus on other problems," Dad advised. "Besides, they were just two kids who had no idea what they were doing."

"Yeah, I think you're right. This whole thing just shows how bad our security really is. We can't even stop an eleven-year-old boy," the man said.

"It's pretty ridiculous. The boys just exposed the flaw," Dad said as craftily as possible.

"Yeah, well, have a good day. By the way, Jack told me the kids' old man looked pretty pissed off," the man said.

"Wouldn't you have been?" Dad asked.

"Yeah I guess I would have. All right, 'bye," the man said.

"Bye," Dad said with relief. Until this day, we have not heard another word about the incident and just assume that the man who called had mixed up the telephone numbers of Bob Koven, and the man that questioned Bobby, Bob Jamison.

"Bomb on Bus"

Anyone who has ever ridden the bus to school understands that the bus is usually not a quiet and calm place. A school bus is a place of agreements and disagreements, play and not work, and a place to make friends and enemies. Because the average bus ride from the East Cobb County stop to Woodruff Academy is usually close to an hour, you can imagine how rambunctious one might become during the ride. Dad did not mind making us ride the bus because the alternative would be to drive twenty six miles south through rush hour traffic every day. Simply waking up to take us to the bus stop on time was a major struggle every morning. I cannot fathom what it would have been like commuting to Woodruff Academy every day and arriving on time.

Like every morning, Dad was racing Bobby and me to the bus. We always caught the bus, but it was usually in the midst of moving or while at a stoplight.

"Where is Dad?" Bobby asked as we sat in the kitchen.

"I don't know, but I woke him up this morning. That man is going to be late for his own funeral," Mom said with a sigh.

It was not much longer before we heard the sound of the stairs bending under Dad's weight. As he ambled into the kitchen, Bobby said, "Dad we've got to get going or we are going to be late."

"I just woke up and I haven't eaten breakfast yet. Go back the car out of the garage while I grab a bite and I'll be right there." Although only in sixth grade, Bobby was already learning how to handle a Chevrolet Suburban.

"You know, if you were not always so late, you wouldn't be so stressed out in the mornings," Mom scolded.

"Would you just hand me a banana or something before I pass out?" Dad said while tying his shoes.

Once Bobby had backed the car out and turned it around in the driveway, Dad and I got in and we departed in the usual hurried fashion. "Move! Get out of the way!" Dad screamed at the other drivers as we swerved between lanes in order to get to the bus stop on time. As we sat waiting at a traffic light near the bus stop, we watched the big yellow school bus pass by going in the opposite direction. "Goddamn it!" Dad hollered as he made an illegal U-turn. We quickly caught up to the bus and when the upcoming traffic light turned red and both vehicles came to a stop, Bobby and I jumped out of our car and ran toward the bus. The bus driver, quite used to this scene, opened the doors to let us in and simultaneously waived to Dad. This was becoming a very regular ritual.

Once onboard, it was chaotic as usual, and I stopped to sit in the middle section of the bus while Bobby continued to the back where the older kids sat. Bobby always had the last seat open for himself because no one else dared to try and take it from him. However, this day was an exception, because there was an unexpected bus rider. A hot blond girl, that Bobby admired, had sat in his seat.

"Hey, Bobby," she said.

"Hey, Lindsay," he replied.

"Do you mind if I sit with you?"

"Not at all," Bobby beamed.

He sat down next to her, and as the bus bounced along the highway, passing through downtown Atlanta, Lindsay and Bobby chatted.

"What's going on?" he asked.

"Not too much. I saw *Speed, the movie,* last weekend," she said.

"I heard that was an awesome movie, but I haven't seen it yet."

"You should go see it some time. Trust me, it's worth it. You know what would be really funny?" asked Lindsay.

"What?"

"If we held up a sign that read, 'Bomb on Bus, if speed declines to 50 mph, we will explode.' It would be like the sign in *Speed*. All of the other cars would back away," she said with a laugh.

"Yeah, that would be pretty funny," Bobby agreed enthusiastically.

Bobby watched as Lindsay pulled a piece of paper out of her book bag and began writing the words. "Would you hold the sign on the back window?" she asked.

"Sure I will," Bobby said as he grabbed the sign. We continued to travel toward school when suddenly all traffic around the bus began to disappear, and a wall of traffic was beginning to form behind us. Soon, the bus was driving alone on I-75 with a barrier of traffic following far behind.

We eventually made it to school, and everything seemed to be fine. Bobby wadded up the sign, threw it into the trashcan at the front of the bus, and went to class as usual. However, by the end of first period, he was called to the principal's office. The principal had him sit down in the chair in front of his desk, and then began by asking, "Mr. Koven, did anything unusual or out of the ordinary happen this morning on the bus?"

Bobby, only remembering Lindsay and not what Lindsay asked him to do, said, "I don't think so. Why?"

The principal said, "Well, let me refresh your memory," and with that, pulled the crinkled sign that Bobby had thrown away, out of his desk drawer. The principal said, "Yes, I and every other member of the administration was quite surprised this morning when the Atlanta Bomb Squad showed up at the bus yard demanding to search Bus #12 for a bomb due to a bomb threat that approximately three hundred motorists reported." Now about to fall out of his chair, Bobby continued to stare and listen in awe. The principal went on, "You have also made my morning much more hectic than usual, mainly due to the fact that I have had to answer hundreds of worried parents' telephone calls about whether or not their child is on the bus with the bomb! Apparently, a radio station picked up the story on the Atlanta Police radio frequency and broadcast the exciting news across the entire city of Atlanta. Mr. Koven, there is no denying the fact that you held the sign because we have proof on the bus 12 videotape."

Bobby, thinking of only how Dad was going react when he heard that his son was making bomb threats, had totally forgotten about Woodruff Academy's bus surveillance system and just continued to stare at the principal.

"What type of punishment are you planning to administer?" Bobby asked tentatively.

"Well, at the moment the plan is to expel you from Woodruff Academy," the principal replied.

"You can't expel me! My parents are going to kill me. Listen, I have worked too hard to get to this school, and my parents have paid too much money for you to simply throw me out of school because of a mistake like this," Bobby protested.

"Well, I'm sorry, Bobby, but this was no little mistake, and expulsion is what will most likely take place. I am going to call your parents after this discussion and you will be notified of your official punishment by the end of the day. Now go back to class," the principal said.

Meanwhile, Dad was on the phone with one of his sisters bragging about Bobby's grades and behavior from his recent semester report, when he received a call waiting interruption signal.

"Carla, he's been great lately," Dad was saying, "I received his semester report card and he had all A's and one B. Not to mention he only received five detentions last semester."

"What an improvement!" Carla said.

"Can you hold on for one second, Woodruff Academy is on the other line?" Dad pressed the "flash" button on the telephone. It was the principal sounding most upset.

"Mr. Koven, there has been a problem concerning your eldest son."

"Jesus, I was just bragging about him. What's the problem?"

"Well, I'm here with the State of Georgia Police as a result of your son's recent behavior on our bus. He held up a sign this morning that basically said that the bus was carrying a bomb, and now we have a real situation as you can imagine," the principal said.

"Well, I can imagine, and I give you permission to punish the living hell out of him," Dad replied, thinking that would be enough to fix the problem.

"As much as I would like to do so, Mr. Koven, we have restrained from any type of disciplinary action here at Woodruff Academy. Instead, the administration is considering expulsion," said the principal.

Dad, dropping his bagel on the floor after hearing this pronouncement, said, "Now, wait a goddamn minute! There's no reason to start considering something that is only going to punish me as the parent. Can't you require him to do some manual labor or community service?"

"We don't feel that even manual labor would be a suitable punishment for such a horrible action taken by your son," the principal said.

"I agree that what Bobby did was bad, but I do not think that it was bad enough to be expelled from school. By the way, if you guys kick him out of school, all you are doing is putting a burden on me. I'll have to go find the boy another school to enroll in, which will not be easy because he will be branded as a troublemaker by you guys," Dad said with anger.

"Mr. Koven, your son "is" a troublemaker."

"Well, goddamn it, if you expel him you'll be pushing him farther down the wrong path in life. You're making a very big mistake and I can promise you that you will regret it," Dad said.

"Is that a threat?" the principal asked.

"It's not a threat, just a promise," Dad said coolly.

As the minutes passed, the argument became much more intense and eventually involved Woodruff Academy's president, headmaster, and a few of the board members. Because of this change, and Dad's quick but extreme threats, Bobby's punishment was reluctantly decreased to a measly two-week suspension from riding the bus. Now, he had to endure the horrible punishment of riding with two varsity cheerleaders each morning, rather than riding the bus as usual. After the calamity was finally sorted out, the entire event turned into a story that Dad laughs about on the phone. At school, Bobby's transgressions only served to give him a bigger and more egotistical reputation.

6

Captain Dad

Whether it was playing sports, learning how to drive, or just attempting to use common sense, Dad was always there to tell us exactly what we were doing right, and mostly what we were doing wrong. As everyone knows, when you are learning how to drive, the most annoying aspect of the process is your parents. They are not just annoying because of their frustrating comments about everything you do while driving, but their behavior, while sitting in the passenger seat, can be even more annoying than their remarks. For example, when my friend would get into the driver's seat, his mother would quickly jump into the passenger's seat, immediately lock the doors, buckle her seat belt, and brace herself with her arms. When they would travel around curves, she would hold on as if they were going to lift off into flight. Because my parents had been planning for the big sixteenth birthday and all it had to offer, they had Bobby and me begin driving by the time we had each reached the age of thirteen. As much as I would like to say it helped, for some reason it did not.

Setting the Wreck Example

Saturday morning is always a time that I enjoy doing absolutely nothing, unless I have to be at a track or cross country meet. Anyway, it was a Saturday morning and I was hoping to spend it leisurely sitting at the kitchen table reading a few magazines and relaxing. However, as soon as I began to hear the rafters squeak, followed by the squeaking of the staircase, and then the final shaking of the house, I had a feeling my plans were about to change rather quickly.

"Gale! I'm going to go to the doctor's office to take care of a few things. I'll be back in a couple hours," Dad shouted through the house as he made his way into the kitchen.

"O.k. honey! Be careful," Mom yelled back.

I tried to hold as still as possible, thinking that maybe he might not see me if I did not move, but I was wrong. I saw one of his eyes catch me in the corner, and then both focused on me. "Matt, what are you up to?"

"Not too much. I was reading a few magazines and taking it easy."

"What do you say about coming with me? I've got a lot to do after my doctor's appointment and I could use your help."

Damn, why me, I thought to myself. "Sure, I need to get out of the house anyway," I said as I stood up and pushed the magazines to the side.

Stepping briskly up into the Suburban, Dad made himself comfortable and added a piece of mail to the stack of papers loosely held by the sun visor. And he wonders why that shit always falls on him while he's driving, I thought to myself as I stepped up into the truck.

"Alright, let's go, we're late." He quickly turned the key in the ignition. The Urban intimidator, otherwise known as Dad, driving his Suburban at high speeds with no recognition or respect for other drivers, pulled out of the driveway with a skid and a honk while simultaneously scraping the mailbox. The mailbox left a long white mark down the entire right side of the vehicle.

"Goddamn!" Dad said as the mailbox scraped by. "Jesus, I'm getting old. Well, I can't do anything about it now," he muttered with embarrassment.

Although somewhat irritated, Dad was not too upset. We continued toward the Interstate. Conditions began to worsen as time passed; traffic was heavy and since we were late, Dad began driving like a maniac.

If Dad is not waving his pistol at other drivers or threatening their lives, he is usually cutting off the nearest driver deliberately and sometimes without even knowing it. When the traffic finally did begin to break up, Dad noticed that a small car with its left turn signal flashing was approaching us from his rear in the right turning lane. Of course, Dad just knew it was "some asshole trying to cut me off" when, in reality, it is usually just another driver who has the same mentality as Dad.

"Do you see that car, Matt?" he asked while pointing in his rear view mirror.

"Yes."

"He's going to try and cut in front of us. By god, it's not going to happen on my watch!" he exclaimed and accelerated.

We managed to stay slightly ahead of the parallel car. The other driver, sensing what was going on, also increased his speed, hoping that he would beat the "asshole in the Suburban" and cut in front of him.

However, with the turning lane's end fast approaching, the driver had to slam on his brakes and attempt to go behind us. "Haha! Look, Matt! We got him!" Dad yelled with joy as the other car fell back and attempted to slip in our lane behind us.

Although it was a good try, it failed miserably because the man's front bumper somehow hooked onto the back of our rear bumper, and when Dad accelerated, he ripped the man's bumper clear off his car. "What was that?" Dad asked.

I quickly turned around to see what had happened, and to my horror I saw the small bumperless car stopped in the road, it's bumper hanging on the back of our departing vehicle. "Dad, you took his bumper!"

"What?" he asked, confused.

"You pulled that man's bumper right off of his car," I said with a laugh.

"Jesus!" Dad said, pulling over to the side of the road and coming to a stop.

Soon afterward, the bumperless car caught up to us and came to a stop a few feet behind us. We all stepped out of our car and approached each other. "Aw no! Look what you did to my car," Dad cried as he pointed to the long white scrape down the side of the Suburban.

"Wow, I didn't realize I did that. How much do think that will cost?" replied the worried man.

"I don't know. I mean between this mark and the scrape that your bumper left on my bumper, it will probably run about five hundred dollars," Dad estimated.

"No problem. By the way my name is Jack Brumbly and I'm training to be a police officer in Atlanta. The last thing I want is another insurance claim against me. My rates are already too high and I don't need anything messing with my driving record right now, if you know what I mean." The man pulled five hundred dollars out of his wallet.

"I completely understand. Insurance is a bitch anyway," Dad replied. "Well, I better be going and I'm really sorry about your car," said the young trainee as he picked up his bumper and threw it in the back of his car. Dad watched the man drive away, shaking his head, amazed with his fabulous "negotiating" abilities.

Little did Dad know what a bad influence his driving was having on Bobby. Bobby was nearing the age of fifteen, the legal age to qualify for a driving permit in Georgia.

The Big Bang

"Watch out!" Dad screamed as we narrowly missed a passing truck. Of course, Bobby was driving. I was sitting in the back seat practicing stress management techniques.

"Would you relax? That truck wasn't that close anyway," Bobby screamed.

"Don't tell me to relax, damn it! How in the hell can I relax when I'm seeing my life flash before my eyes every five minutes? It's definitely going to be a while before you drive again. As a matter of fact, I think you should just pull over right now and let me take control," Dad barked. I tried not to make a sound as I sighed with relief.

"Maybe Dad's right," I said.

"Jesus, you guys are the biggest scaredy cats," Bobby retorted. He maneuvered the car to the side of the road and slammed on the brakes.

"It's better to be a scaredy cat than a dead cat," Dad countered.

I couldn't wait for Bobby to turn fifteen and legally become eligible for a permit. He had been driving for about a year now, and under the close supervision of Dad, his driving was slowly improving. However, it was never quite perfect-ever!

It was now a year and a half after the above incident and Bobby was sixteen. Because we woke up late, we were in a hurry to get to school, like every morning, and the driving conditions were horrible. Bobby, knowing that nothing could possibly go wrong, was in the midst of his usual road rage and constantly switching lanes to pass people while flashing his lights at the victimized drivers in the pouring rain.

"Get out of the way, you idiot!" he screamed at one driver. "Everyone freaks out when a little water gets on the road. I don't understand," he said as he shifted the windshield wipers to the maximum speed.

He had been driving for about six months on his own and by this time I was used to the constant jerking and braking, so I began to study for a science test while riding in the passenger seat. We were about halfway to school when our Dodge Durango went into a hydroplaning spin. Bobby had jerked the car into a different lane of traffic in order to avoid a quickly oncoming car that was close to being stopped. The result of the sudden movement caused the car to begin to fishtail while hydroplaning. As I felt the back of the car begin to slide sideways across the Interstate, I yelled, "We're fucked!"

Bobby quickly looked at me and said, "Hold on!" He tried to turn into the skid in order to gain control, but his attempt failed and the car began to spin. We somehow spun across four lanes of traffic at 65 mph without hitting another car, but then we both noticed the rapidly approaching median wall.

It was my side of the car that was going to hit the wall, and once Bobby realized this fact, he faced me with a worried look and said, "Matt, hold on for your life." The SUV smashed into the median wall, scattering my precious science cards all across I-285. When the Durango finally came to a stop, all of the doors were jammed, every window except two were blown out, and all but one side of the car was smashed completely inward.

"Jesus Christ! Are you o.k.?" he asked me.

"Yeah, I'm fine. Did we hit anyone?"

"I'm not sure. I don't think so. Dad's going to be so pissed." I'd never seen him look so worried.

"He'll probably be pretty mad," I said, unbuckling my seatbelt. We both crawled through the windows and once we were both standing outside the demolished vehicle, it started raining. Bobby figured that it was time to call Dad.

He dialed the number on his cell phone. As I heard Dad's voice saying "hello" on the other end of the line, Bobby's facial expression turned to one of extreme sorrow.

"Hey, Dad, it's Bobby," he said in a weak voice.

"Hey buddy, is something wrong?" Dad asked intuitively.

"Yes, I wrecked the car," Bobby said.

"Are you guys alright?" Dad asked.

"Yes, I'm o.k. and Matt's alright, too. Dad, the car is totally screwed."

"Don't worry about the goddamn car. Jesus, where are you?" Dad asked.

"In the inside emergency lane of I-285 before the I-20 exit," Bobby said.

"Well, goddamnit, I'll be there as fast as I can. Just sit tight, and if a wrecker comes, don't let him tow the car until I get there! Got it?"

"Yeah, got it. Dad, I'm really sorry," Bobby looked extremely grim.

"Me too," Dad said as he hung up the phone.

After hanging up the phone, Bobby suddenly went ballistic. He began to kick the side of the destroyed Durango, and after cursing for a good five minutes, he picked up a dislodged fog light that was covered in antifreeze, and smashed it on the ground. I said wearily, "You might at least be able to use the fog lights for something else."

"Shut the hell up! Dad is going to fucking murder me when he sees this car," yelled Bobby.

"Yeah probably," I said as I noticed an oncoming patrol car.

"I told him it was screwed, but I don't think he knows how bad it really looks," Bobby said.

The oncoming patrol car came to a stop behind our disaster. A black police officer stepped out of his car and walked toward us.

"Damn!" the officer said, studying the car. After looking at the car for about a minute, the officer approached us. "Which one of you crazy fools was driving?" the officer asked.

"I was," Bobby uttered.

"Let me see your driver's license young man," the officer demanded. Bobby handed the officer his license and began to explain what had happened. He emphasized the fact that he was not speeding, but the officer looked at him as if he was just another sixteen-year-old that who just added another number to the dangerous teenage driving statistic. Once we assured the officer that we were okay, he left, and Bobby phoned Dad again.

"Where are you?" Bobby asked when Dad came on the line.

"Where am I? I'm sitting in your goddamn traffic jam! You've backed the highway up to kingdom come. Just stay there. It'll will take me about fifteen minutes," Dad bellowed.

"It's not like I'm going to drive away," Bobby said and hung up the phone. The wrecker arrived at about the same time as Dad. It was now beginning to rain much harder. Both the wrecker truck driver and Dad approached the Durango at relatively the same time.

"My God! All I can say is that you guys better count your blessings," Dad said, looking at the car.

"I'll go ahead and hook her up," the wrecker driver said. "You can have it picked up at the wrecking site."

"I think you should go ahead and take it straight to the dealership," Dad said.

"I'm sorry Mister, but that's not the way we do it," the man said.

"Listen, you would really be helping a devastated father out if you took it to the dealership. Here's fifty bucks for your extra trouble," Dad said, handing the man a fifty-dollar bill.

The man stared at the bill for a moment and then at the Durango. "Alright, you guys seem to be nice people. I don't need this," he said and gave the fifty-dollar bill back to Dad.

We watched the wrecked SUV being towed away in the rain. "You guys were so lucky," Dad said.

"I know," Bobby said humbly.

"Don't worry about it, son. I'm just glad that you guys are safe, even if it doubles my insurance premiums for the next six years," Dad said with a sigh. "All right, let's go."

"Where are we going?" I asked.

"To school. Don't think that a little incident like this is going to get you out of going to school. Get your asses in my car and shut up!" Dad said.

We piled into Dad's Suburban and he drove us to school. Even though most kids would have been taken home after a wreck like this, Dad did not hesitate about making us go through the rest of the day taking our tests with only the images of I-285 spinning in our heads instead of algorithms and formulas. The next day we riding on the big yellow bus, and it stayed that way for the rest of the year.

Like Father Like Son

If there was a highlight of Bobby's first wreck, it was that there was no one else involved. When Bobby finally struck a deal with Dad to get another Durango about six months later, he would not have the same good fortune with his future wrecks. All his upcoming accidents always included a very non-cooperating individual. In short, Bobby should have been taking notes from Dad during the delicate time of negotiating with the other people involved in a wreck that was usually Dad's fault. If you negotiate properly, you could convince the other person not to notify their insurance agency, get a least three quotes to fix the damage, and then simply pay the person in cash without any other hassles, such as, insurance rates increasing or dealing with a police officer.

With all of these skills developed, Bobby was on his way to having another wreck at about eleven in the morning during the summer following his junior year in high school. Dad had taken me to a doctor's appointment and Bobby had planned to meet us at a CVS Pharmacy that was near my doctor's office. For once in our lives, Dad and I were actually early for my appointment. We walked into the waiting room and signed in with five minutes to spare.

After signing my name on the sheet at the front desk, we both sat down in the waiting room and waited. Soon, the thirty-minute mark began to tick by, and it was at about the same time that Dad began his waiting room lecture. "It's been thirty minutes since we got here on time, and we're still waiting! I can't take these doctors any longer. All they do is make you come to an appointment, and then fucking lock you in a waiting room for another hour until they can get their own ass caught back up on time and finally see you! I-," then his cell phone rang. "Hello," he said.

"Hey, Dad, it's Bobby."

"Hey, buddy! What's going on?"

"Well, I've kinda got some bad news. You see I was over here waiting on you guys at the CVS, but I was pulling into the parking lot and accidentally scraped another man's bumper. It's basically a damn tire mark but the guy is going ballistic over it," Bobby said shakily.

"Damn it, Bobby, what in the hell do you want me to do about it?" Dad snapped. "I've been over here boiling in this goddamn waiting room for half an hour and you want me to get up and walk out just to go fix your fuckup. Well, I can't, but I'll be there as soon as I can. Meantime, try not to screw anything else up." Everyone in the waiting room was now staring at us after Dad hung up the phone. Over the years, I have learned to deal with situations like this quite well, and I believe that I have lost the ability to be embarrassed over any situation.

While we continued to wait for the doctor, Bobby was trying to negotiate with the man whose bumper was bruised.

"Listen, sir, I can't tell you how sorry I am for this inconvenience, but I think it would benefit both our interests not to call the police or notify our insurance companies," Bobby said politely.

"I don't know. I think I want to have your insurance company cover this, and maybe call the authorities," the man said.

"Look, the damage is basically a tire mark. If you call your insurance agency, they will cover the damage, but they will also raise your premiums, as well as mine. If the police come, then one of us will most likely get a ticket, and a report will have to be filed. I'm not trying to cheat you out of anything, I'm just trying to make both of our lives easier," Bobby explained.

"I guess you have a point," the man said.

"I know I have a point," Bobby said.

"Well, you've convinced me not to notify the authorities or my insurance. So, what do you want me to do?" he asked.

"Well, the first thing to do is to go to a few collision repair garages and get a couple of quotes on how much the damage will cost to fix. I feel like you are an honest guy, so you call me and tell me what the quotes are, and we will decide on an amount. Then, I will pay you directly," Bobby said confidently.

"That sounds like a good plan, but what about my time spent looking for a garage?" the man asked.

"What do mean?" Bobby inquired.

"I mean, why shouldn't I get paid something for spending my time? Frankly, if you had not hit me, I would not be wasting my time looking for a garage to fix my car," the man said.

"Well, shit happens," Bobby said nonchalantly.

"Yeah, shit does happen. Maybe I'll go ahead and call my insurance agency," the man began to say.

"Fine, my father's going to be here soon and I really do not want him to get in the middle of this. How much do you want extra?" Bobby asked.

"I think a hundred and fifty dollars will do it," the man said.

"Hell no, are you crazy?"

"All right, how about a hundred dollars?"

"It's a deal."

Dad and I had finished with the doctor and we were on our way to the CVS Pharmacy just as Bobby and the man were departing from their negations with each other. Dad, already having thought of every possible thing to say, approached the man.

"Hi, I'm Bob Koven," Dad said as he stuck out his hand.

"I'm Jim Pitts," the man said with a nod.

"I see my son has inconvenienced you quite a bit."

"Yes, he has a little, but we've worked something out."

"Oh really?" Dad responded. The man explained what had happened and the deal that he and Bobby had struck. Everything was going fine until Dad heard him say that Bobby would pay him one hundred dollars for his extra troubles. "A hundred dollars? Are you serious?" Dad roared.

"Why yes, I am serious. This is going to affect my schedule for the day. Especially since I have to find a garage to give me a quote on this damage," replied the man.

"I don't really give a fuck about your schedule. Look, you can both get a quote on the damage and I will gladly pay you for it, or you can go to hell and report a goddamn fifty-dollar wreck to your insurance agency. But, there is no way in hell that I'm going to pay you for your time because your time means nothing to me," Dad fumed.

"Well, sir, I don't really appreciate your tone, but if you insist, I shall notify my insurance company and you will be hearing from me in the next week," the man said.

"Why don't you just go stick it up your ass, you little sonofabitch!" Dad screamed at the man, who quickly got back into his car and drove away.

Bobby watched the man's departing car and turned to Dad.

"You ruined it!"

"No, I didn't! Dad shouted. "The man was a weasel anyway. He would have lied about the repair and we would have probably paid double. By the way, if it were not for your ignorant driving, we wouldn't be standing here." Bobby just stood there with his mouth open in awe, wondering why his dad acts like a psycho whenever he does something right. When we all got into Bobby's car, Dad said, "Boys, you can't let other people take advantage of you no matter how great the payback or benefit is."

Although Dad felt like he had taken the correct action, our car insurance premiums increased the next month. However, as long as an individual truly believes in is decision, then it is impossible to persuade him otherwise.

7

Family Time

A phrase that Dad almost lives by is one that I once saw on a sign hanging on a house. It read, "Friends always welcome. Relatives by appointment only." This is probably due to the fact that our family is, in a word, dysfunctional. I had no idea that communication existed without screaming until I began visiting and staying with friends' families and discovered that it is possible to have a confrontation without making an enormous "scene." Odd things always seemed to happen to my family that usually did not happen to other families. I later figured out that it was my family's behavior that caused so many out of the ordinary events to occur.

The Iowa Odyssey

It was that time of year again -Christmas break- and we had to make that "goddamn eight million mile trip to Iowa," as Dad referred to it. It was my grandparents' 50th anniversary, and the date was the talk of the town in Lone Tree, Iowa. Commercially, Lone Tree consists of about two and a half streets of small buildings, and the rest is acres and acres of corn and bean fields. However, during Christmas break there are no crops, only gigantic drifts of snow, and forecasts that call for a high of ten degrees. The drive from Atlanta to Lone Tree takes approximately forever, and by the time you get there, you feel like dying, mainly due to the blood clots that have formed in your legs. Besides this hardship and becoming a chain smoker overnight, it is nice to see my grandparents and other family members who have already traveled to Lone Tree or live there.

This year would be a little different because Dad had bigger plans than to just visit his in-laws for their anniversary. He and Bobby, would drive one car each to Paducah, Kentucky, where they would leave one of the cars at my aunt's house and continue the journey in the other car. Mom and I would fly to Iowa two days after they left, due to an English exam that I had to take, and meet them at the airport in Cedar Rapids, Iowa. After the anniversary party weekend, we would all drive back to Kentucky where Mom would take the other car home, and Dad, Bobby, and me would travel onto Real Foot Lake, Tennessee to hunt ducks for four days. Interesting things were bound to happen during this winter vacation.

When Mom and I arrived at the airport in Cedar Rapids, Iowa, we went straight to the baggage claim area where we waited for our dependable ride to pick us up. As the five-minute mark was beginning to tick by, I noticed what looked like a drunk driver heading in our direction. I pointed out the swerving car to Mom, who said, "That's just your father, honey." When I took a second look, I realized that it *was* my father, careening around the curves and running over orange cones, while trying to maneuver on the icy road. Once in the car, Dad was still complaining about the long drive just as he was when he left Atlanta, and I wondered how Bobby ever made the trip.

"I really don't understand, Gale, why do your parents still want to live in the Arctic Circle?" Dad asked mockingly.

"Now don't be silly, honey. They don't live in the Arctic Circle," Mom said.

"It might as well be. Look! The temperature gauge on the car is stuck on 'Ice.' It's so cold that it won't even read a temperature."

"Bob, you should really quit complaining. I read an article in the *Oprah magazine* that said complaining is one of the major symptoms of general depression. If a person persistently complains, it's a sign of an unhealthy mental state."

"You want to know something that is going to make me unhealthier?" Dad asked.

"What?" Mom said

"The air quality of your parents' house," Dad said with a laugh.

It started to snow again while we were traveling toward my grandparents' house and as we began to increase our speed, I heard a progressively louder noise. It sounded like something scraping against the pavement.

"Dad, what is that sound?" I asked nervously.

"Matt, that's the sound of driving on ice. You've been living in The South and don't understand what it's like to drive in real winter weather."

It was right at that moment that a loud pop sound was heard and as I looked back, I saw an orange cone flying through the air. The cone smashed into the hood of another car, and caused the driver to fishtail off the road. I was the only one who noticed the event, so we kept driving. But at least there was no more scraping sound.

When Dad put the Suburban in "park" and turned the engine off in front of my grandparents' house, he just sat there staring. I asked, "What's wrong?"

"I'm just preparing myself for seven days of no privacy and no air," he said.

I laughed and stepped out of the car into the blistering five-degree wind. We all fought our way to the front door and rang the bell. When the door flew open, a wave of heat and smoke hit us with such force that it knocked us all backwards.

My grandmother, Sue Smothers, grinned at us and said, "Hey, guys! Come on in, the party's just getting started! Matt you have gotten so big, and Bobby! I can't believe my eyes; you look just like a college boy."

Bobby and I just stared at each other while Grandma continued to talk and ask if we wanted to join in the Yatzee game. We all slept well that night. However, Mom and Dad were having a hard time on the thirty-year-old box spring mattress that was on their bed, and we all woke up every morning with a congested head and nose due to the smoke.

Bobby and I spent the next day walking the harvested crop fields to look for wild pheasant, while Dad drove all over Iowa looking for a single box spring mattress. Finally, he found an old mattress store in downtown Iowa City, where, first he became best friends with the mattress sales representative, Pete, and then began to bargain about the price. After getting to know each other, Dad said, "So, can you make me an offer on this mattress?"

Even though the price tag was in plain view, Pete looked at Dad and said, "I don't know, I mean we already mark our mattresses down so that the price is so low that it's not really possible to give any discounts."

"Well, Pete, if you go and look up my name in your computer, you'll see that I've bought countless mattresses from this fine store, and in the past, I've always been given a discount of some type, usually a builder's discount."

Pete, not wanting to call Dad's bluff said, "I totally understand, Mr. Koven, and because we certainly do not want to lose a distinguished customer as yourself, I'll knock fifteen percent off the retail price."

"I would sure appreciate that, and if you don't mind, could you have your boys in the back tie it to the roof of my car?"

"No problem. And, Mr. Koven, it was a pleasure doing business with you," Pete said. As Dad thought to himself about what a genius he was, the men from the back of the store tied the mattress to the roof of the small jeep Cherokee with twine, the only available rope in the store.

Now, anybody with the brain of a mouse has the common sense not to tie a hundred-pound box mattress to a roof of a car using twine. The truth was that the man in the mattress store was so scared to tell Dad that they did not have rope that he told his boys to use whatever they had in the store. When Dad began to accelerate down the highway, the twine began to unravel, and soon the mattress was simply lying, untethered, on top of the car. At about the 75 mph mark, Dad heard a quick sliding sound from the roof, and as he looked into his rear-view mirror, he saw the "goddamn" mattress soaring through the air and headed straight for an eighteen-wheeler. Right as Dad was beginning his next sentence with, "That mother-f…..!" the huge truck smashed straight through the mattress, and as Dad continued his dramatic monologue, springs, wood, and metal exploded onto the highway. Dad quickly began to move over to the emergency lane, decelerate, while simultaneously watching approaching cars hit the metal springs, and blow their tires out. Next, Dad promptly dialed 911 and said, "There is a mattress lying in the middle of the roadway outside of Iowa City, and it's causing cars and trucks to skid off the road!"

The emergency response woman asked, "Sir, did you by any chance see what vehicle the mattress originated from and write down the license plate number?"

"No, I did not," Dad replied as he hung up the phone and started to drive back to the house. As Dad broke through the wall of smoke when he came through the front door, everyone looked at him and said in unison, "Where's the new mattress?"

"It's on the goddamn highway and if you don't believe me, here's the damn receipt!" Dad replied.

Not ever caring too much about the whole mattress business anyway, Grandma said, "Well, how about a tuna fish sandwich, Bob?"

Dad was incredulous. "Sue, you fed me breakfast and lunch before I left and it's only two o'clock. How many damn times do you all eat in a single day up here?"

"Now there's no need to get grumpy over a lousy mattress. You'll probably feel better after eating something," Grandma insisted.

"No, the problem is that all you do up here is eat and sleep, and when I can't sleep because I'm rolling around like a goddamn sardine on a fifty-year-old box mattress, all I am able to do is eat all day long and feel like shit," Dad also insisted. The room was silent, but as soon as Dad left to go downstairs, the Yatzee and gin rummy games continued.

The next morning I woke up early, like every morning, to run in order to stay in shape and train for the upcoming Track and Field season in the spring. However, this morning was a little windier and colder than the previous ones, around five below to be exact, but I continued to stretch and think about how I would pass the time while running the next twelve miles. An hour and twenty-four minutes later, I could not feel anything on my body, and as I came through the front door, the curtain of smoke was enough to knock me unconscious. I was to wake up two hours later caught in the middle of a lecture that was directed toward me. It was Dad, of course, and it was fundamentally about the same point: how stupid I was to go running in the cold, just reiterated over and over using different words. "Are you dense, Matt?" Dad asked as I was coming to my senses.

"No, I just didn't think it would be that cold outside and" I was saying as Dad cut me short.

"That's exactly right. You didn't think. My God, what do I have to do to get you and your brother to start thinking? If the temperature is below zero, then you don't go for a joyful twelve mile run," Finally, when his diatribe was finished, he said, "Well, maybe I can't blame you. I'd probably run twelve miles in sub-zero weather to escape the smoke, too." I laughed and he told me to get my ass up because we were going pheasant hunting that morning.

Bobby, Dad, and I dressed for the hunt, grabbed our gear and headed for Grandpa's El Camino. Cars must not have been built to hold a lot of weight back in the El Camino days, because when all three of us stuffed ourselves into the car, it bottomed out while still in "park." Of course, we did not realize this at the time and while Dad was saying, "Boys, this is the way good cars used to be built," he threw the gear shift into reverse and dragged the car on its floor boards all the way out of the garage. "This fucking piece of shit car," Dad shouted.

"I thought this was a good car like back in the old days," Bobby said with a loud laugh.

"Shut the hell up, you fuck!" Dad said. Bobby looked at our father with surprise.

"Yeah, I'm talking to you, now go get the goddamn Suburban so we can get the hell out of here," Dad ordered.

As Bobby started toward the Suburban he began to sing, "It's a Holly Jolly Christmas, it's the best time of the year........."

"Matt, your brother is nothing but a smartass, you know?"

"I know."

After loading the Suburban and driving a couple of miles down a straight road, we came to what seemed to be a completely random spot and stopped.

"O.k.! Everybody out," Dad enthusiastically announced.

We began to walk near fence posts and along the ditches of the deserted road, hoping to scare wild pheasant out of the weeds and into the air. It seemed that about every five minutes one or two pheasant would get up out of the weeds, but they would get up almost a quarter of mile in front of us. It was ridiculous how smart the late season surviving birds appeared to be. Even Dad remarked, "These are the smartest pheasants I have ever seen."

Bobby and I agreed with him, both of us laughing throughout the hunt.

We walked about four miles through the icy wind, and when we all decided that we had frozen enough for one day, we began to head back to the house. However, on the way back to the car Dad had to relieve himself and told us to keep moving, and that he would catch up with us. About forty seconds later, Bobby and I unsuspectingly scared up one last pheasant. The pheasant got up closer than usual, but it was too fast for Bobby and me. We noticed that the bird began to fly in the direction of Dad, who was camouflaged among the tall grass. We called out, "Dad! There's one coming to you."

With only one hand available, Dad picked up his shotgun, shouldered it, took aim, and fired. The pheasant fell only a few feet away from him. "Did you guys see that?" he said. Bobby and I stared awestruck.

"Yeah, we saw it," I said as we turned around and headed back to the car with amazed laughter.

Once back to our favorite air-free environment, everyone was in a hurry, now trying to get ready for the big 50th anniversary celebration that night at a hotel dining room. While Dad raced to get dressed, which is quite a task, I was being given strict directions on how to use my grandma's camera. I was told, "You must take pictures of Aunt Jenny with Uncle Steve, and don't forget about Jack and Jim." By the time Grandma had finished her photography instructions and warnings, I had about five minutes to get dressed. With my grandmother nervous as a cat and worrying about every detail and my grandfather already starting on his first gin and tonic, we were off to the celebration. The hotel dining room looked like a scene from *Grumpy Old Men*, but there was an open bar and everyone was having a great time. After finishing my responsibility -taking pictures of drunken family members- I noticed an attractive girl sitting at a table near the bar. It was only after trying to flirt with her that I found out she was my second cousin. In fact, I met about ten cousins that I never knew existed. As the party began to wind down, Bobby and I began the job of having to make sure everyone made it safely to whatever mode of transportation they were taking home. We arrived home at about midnight, and as I got into bed, I could already hear Dad beginning to curse about the box spring mattress that he had failed to replace.

Finally, it was time to go home and you would have thought Dad had won the lottery. The drive back to Paducah, Kentucky, included Dad's long monologue about how he could finally breathe and about the events that took place in the past week. As we pulled out of the driveway and began traveling down the road, I pulled out one of my inhalers that I had forgotten to use that morning. When Dad noticed the inhaler he said, "Matt, let me see that thing."

"Sure," I said, handing it to him.

After taking about four puffs and inhaling deeply, he sighed and shouted happily, "Goddamn, it feels good to breathe!"

"Now don't act like you're already feeling better. You've only been out of that house for ten minutes," Mom said.

"You're right! And it already makes all the difference in the world." Dad let out a hearty laugh and headed south.

After a good spirited road trip, we arrived at my aunt's house in Paducah, Kentucky. We began to say our goodbyes to Mom, who was taking the other car home, when she began her usual speech. "Now remember boys: No messing around with guns and alcohol. Matt, there better not be any drinking "cough syrup" or dangerous horse playing."

"There won't be," Bobby and I promised as we hugged her goodbye and left.

Dad, Bobby, and I were now back on the road and getting into our hunting mode. This "mode" is when whatever is talked about is never taken seriously whether jokes, complaints, name-calling, or whatever other stupid conversation is started. Bobby was in charge of the map and had found a route that should have saved us about an hour of driving. With Bobby's directions and the professional-grade driving/road rage of Dad, we blazed along the highway for about five hours when Bobby demanded that we exit. The road eventually narrowed down to a gravel path and Dad said, "Are you sure that this road is going to cross the Mississippi into Tennessee?"

Bobby nodded. "The map shows this road crossing in about a mile; just keep going." Soon after, we spotted two men on four-wheelers and stopped them to ask where the road leads.

"Does this road ever cross the Mississippi?" Dad asked.

"It should, but I haven't been all the way down this road in a long time," replied one of the men. After saying thanks, we headed further down the road and eventually did come to the river. The road dead-ended into a ferry crossing with a sign that read, "Closed for safety precautions [January 1993]."

"Bobby, you goddamn idiot! What the hell is wrong with you, and don't tell me the map is wrong because I know you're the goddamn idiot," Dad bellowed.

"I thought," Bobby began to say as Dad cut him off with, "You didn't goddamn think because if you did, we wouldn't be sitting here looking at a fucking river without a road!" As the arguing continued, Dad turned the car around and hustled back to the main highway, which was about thirty miles from where we were. While passing and spraying the original two men on the four-wheelers with dirt and mud, I began to think about the upcoming hunt.

We planned to meet the Harris boys, Mr. Harris and his two sons, at Reel Foot Lake, Tennessee like we did every year. Some years other friends such as the Hutchinson boys would join us as well. However, no matter who showed up to hunt, it always seemed that the Harris and Koven boys found each other's company. In order to understand the relationship between Dad and his friends, let me explain. Whether in high school or later in life, everyone usually has a close group of friends that are always there for you when you need them. Dad has had many friends, but only a small group of close friends. This group of men is almost like a constantly competing Boy Scout pack. If one person buys a Suburban that is newer than his friends' Suburbans, everyone else goes out and buys the most recent Suburban model. During quail season, if one man has a better shotgun than the rest, everyone first makes fun of the man for spending the extra money on the gun, and then they shop non-stop to find the same or better shotgun. When one of the men builds a lake house, the others build a bigger lake house, and so the cycle continues. Besides constantly competing over who has the newer and superior article, there are daily phone calls that only concern, "How much so and so spent on whatever." If there was no image to match with the people speaking in the conversations and constant gossiping, it would probably sound like a bunch of women at a social club. Between morale boosting conversations and regular scout trips, Dad's friends were always there whether it was in a time of need, or simply trying to plan a trip for the opening day of duck season.

Ducks Unlimited

We finally made it to the Blue Bank Inn, located on Reel Foot Lake and in the town of Samberg, Tennessee. After checking in at the front desk and receiving the keys to our private cabin, we unpacked the car and settled into our temporary home. Although there were three bedrooms: one with a single queen size bed, and the other two with double bunk beds, Mr. Harris and Dad both had their own bedroom because of their horrible snoring problems. That left one bedroom for the four sons. Although this arrangement did not make sense, it was worth it once the snoring began.

Finally, Mr. Harris and his two sons, Russell and Jeffery, arrived. "Hey buddy!" Harris said, greeting Dad with an outstretched hand.

"How was the drive?" Dad asked

"Long as hell. I swear every year it gets harder. By the time we get here I feel like an old fart," Harris said.

"Well, you are starting to look old, especially with those big glasses you wear. They're so thick that in ten years you might as well be wearing coke bottles," Dad joked.

"Whatever, Mr. Peavey," Harris said. I'm not sure when Dad was given the nickname Mr. Peavey, but he was stuck with it for a long time. After we all got reacquainted with each other, the joking, name-calling, and endless conversation began and didn't stop until the end of the trip. As usual, we all got to bed too late, and right on cue, Dad and Harris's snoring enveloped the entire cabin.

"Get up, goddamn it! Everyone up right now; we're late as hell!" Dad screamed at 3:00 a.m. It was one of those anticipated mornings before a duck hunt that I had waited for all year, but Dad had forgotten to set his watch back now that we were in a new time zone. As I began to scramble to my feet, I remembered the remote control fart machine that I had planted in Harris's bed to wake him up with. I quickly grabbed the remote control and pressed the button, which sounded a loud fart that could be heard through the wall. The fart was so loud that it not only woke Mr. Harris out of his coma-like sleep, but it caused him to sit up so fast that he smashed his head into the rafters of the bunk bed above him and nearly gave him a concussion. "That little bastard!" he yelped in pain. It was about this time that everyone realized we were up too early and that Dad had made a mistake.

"Mr. Koven," Russell said.

"Yes, Russell," Dad said.

"According to my watch, it's one hour too early," Russell politely replied.

"Well, goddamn! I'm sorry, guys, it's my fault. Go back to bed cause we got to be up in an hour," Dad instructed.

"Jesus Christ, Mr. Peavey! If anybody was going to fuck up, you know it was going to be him," Harris joked as he stood in his underwear, rubbing his sore forehead. After everyone finally stopped complaining, we all decided to go back to sleep for another hour or so. Although this was a good idea, it too, failed because we forgot to reset the alarm clock. Thankfully, Bobby happened to haphazardly wake up and look at the time. We were now an hour and a half late, which meant we would have to skip breakfast and haul ass over to the loading ramp where our duck guide, David, was waiting. Of course, David was already waiting at the ramp with a disgusted grin on his face. Due to his forgetful "clienteles" he had to sit there by himself and watch every other guide load their boats into the water and head out to the timber to kill those "goddamn ducks" with dependable clients.

"Where in the flying fuck have y'all been!?" yelled David. "We're not going to kill any ducks with fuckers like you in the water. Let's go!" We all just stood there for a second, but eventually started moving and loaded the boat to go to the blind.

After making the grueling thirty-minute trip across the lake in the freezing cold, and pitch black darkness, we approached the duck blind. This year the lake had so much rain that it was about two feet higher than usual, which caused the blind to slightly flood. Because of this difficulty, the boat would not fit in the little garage behind the blind, and we could not use the door either. Instead, the boat had to be tied off on the side of the blind, and everyone had to enter the blind by climbing over the side, walking across the roof, and sliding into one of the head holes. Although this does not sound like a complicated task, it is a nearly impossible one for a large individual. Bobby and I were the first to slip into the blind, and once inside we began to turn on the lights, gas, and other fixtures. I had volunteered to go first because I really did not want to be around when it was Dad and Mr. Harris's turn. As I was bending down to find the gas line, I heard Dad cursing as he was climbing on the roof, but once there, I began to here the rafters crack and bend under his weight as he made his way across the roof. I believe that it was approximately when I heard the loud snap that I jumped out of the way just in time for Dad to come crashing through the roof, shotgun and all. The first person to speak was the guide, David, and he said, "Goddamnit, Bob! Your fat ass is going to scare all the ducks away."

"Well, goddamn it! God forbid that there be anybody to help me get into this motherfucking hell hole!" Dad shrieked as he maneuvered himself into the blind.

"Jesus, Mr. Peavey, are you going to make it down there?" Harris asked, shaking with laughter.

As everyone tried not to laugh too much, Dad said, "Yeah, just keep laughing. We'll see who can shoot the ducks," he said.

As we waited for the sun to slowly rise, Dad began to cook biscuits in the old oven in the back of the blind. Although everyone was very hungry and happy that the biscuits were being cooked, they all still gave Dad hell for cooking. They would jokingly say, "How are the biscuits doing down there, Mr. Peavey? Are you going to bake any cakes when you're through?"

"Y'all aren't going to get any biscuits if you don't shut the hell up!" Dad would reply from the back of the blind. Nevertheless, when the ducks began to fly, Dad always got back up to the front of the blind ready for action. When a group of ducks would fly in our direction, we would all be caught sitting on our haunches without any support but our own legs. I know this action does not sound hard, but after about five minutes it becomes a pretty challenging position to hold. David would say excitedly, "Boys, there's a group coming in from left. Hold still............. alright now, ease down."

As we all were knelt down and not moving, David began calling ducks using one of his many duck calls. As soon as five minutes had passed, the fatigued Mr. Harris and Dad began to complain. "Jesus, I don't think I can feel my legs anymore," Mr. Harris grumbled.

"Yeah, me too," Dad said. "David, if you can't get these ducks to land in the next minute, I think my knees are going to give out."

"Just hold on! If you old farts would quit complaining for five seconds, I might be able to get some ducks in here," David was definitely annoyed.

Finally, the ducks flew into our water hole and the result was absolutely worth the wait. However, when Dad did cook in the blind, it was always at the exact moment when everyone had started to eat whatever he had cooked that a group of ducks would pitch toward our water hole and dive inward. This would cause much confusion within the blind because everyone was usually so hungry they did not want to throw away the food, but also anxious not to let a duck get away. This situation was usually resolved in seconds and everyone would be standing up shooting, while simultaneously, holding whatever food item they had in their mouth. Having watched this method of shooting for many years, there finally came a day when I was caught in the same predicament and had to make use of the same technique. It is because of my own experience that I understand how Dad lost his glasses while shooting/eating. Since the blind was flooded, finding the glasses proved to be a more challenging task than anyone had imagined. However, by early afternoon the glasses were found and Dad miraculously shot just as many ducks as the rest of us.

Following a few more days of similar activities it was time to go home. "Thank you Mr. Harris, I had a wonderful time," I said, holding out my hand. "By the way, I really am sorry about the head injury."

"No problem. Just keep an eye on the old man, and hopefully we'll see each other soon," Harris said with a smile as he shook my hand.

The two Suburbans pulled out of the Blue Bank Inn and headed toward Atlanta. My winter break had already gotten off to an unusual start, and I looked forward to spending the rest of it at home with no more surprises.

8

Summer Vacation

Summer vacation is a time of excitement and a time of boredom, a time of freedom and a time of restraints, a time of bonding closer to your parents and time of trying to get the hell away from them. Having been given the responsibility to watch Bobby and me since mom worked outside the home, Dad held up pretty well, for the first month. However, it was always around the time that the first month ended that Dad began to get a little anxious and tired of his babysitting responsibilities. He was always running some type of business, doing business deals, or just trying to get something done, while simultaneously, looking after us. Again, after the first month of having to put up with us and our success in pushing him well beyond his limit, that he would try to find and create jobs for us to keep us "out of his hair."

Getting To Work

By the time I graduated from the first grade, I had already learned my share of how business was conducted. Dad had us parking cars for the Bellsouth Classic PGA Tournament before I could read. Bobby and I did not mind it at all. In a quick three days of work we would easily bring in a hefty $2,000. The next year Bobby proposed an ingenious idea of raising the price. We quickly doubled our profits. However, because the tournament moved to a different country club and only lasted three days per year, Dad needed to find us another place to keep us busy, yet productive and involved in business.

Working in my parents' business seemed to provide a sensible solution. They owned Discovery Zone, a 12,000 square foot indoor playground, which served as a safe haven for soccer moms and their children. Taking their kids to Discovery Zone did not require much effort and the result would be that their child became very tired, therefore, more than willing to go to bed once at home. Discovery Zone was filled with tunnels to crawl through, ball pens to play in, and video games to play. Although there were more than three locations around Atlanta, after the first year of going to Discovery Zone every day after school and having more than three of my birthday parties located there, they all were basically the same. Throughout the entire Discover Zone experience, Dad was constantly on edge. First, IBM and the rest of the world would not quit reiterating the fact that computers were necessary when running a business in the '90s. Of course, Dad understood this, but being the most computer illiterate person imaginable, he did not really understand the true need for computers. Finally, and after much consideration, Dad decided to order his computers from IBM.

The new computers arrived within a matter of days. They were being set up and plugged into the walls of an office within one of the stores, Dad remarked that the computers looked and weighed more like tanks than useful equipment. By the end of the day the servicemen were gone and Dad was left staring at the new machines in awe. "Well, I guess I'm now up to date. No more taking shit from those IBM geeks," Dad said as he left the office.

The next day, Dad decided to see how the new equipment worked. Sitting alone in the office, he began by pressing the power button on the big tower unit and on the monitor. "That was easy enough," Dad said. He then began to fumble with the mouse. "What the hell does this gadget do?" he said as Mom entered the office.

"Honey, that's called a mouse. You use it to move the little pointer around the screen and click on different programs or functions."

As messages began to pop up on the monitor due to a constant clicking of the right mouse button, Dad became frustrated and confused, "What in the hell is going on?" His foot now accidentally put enough pressure on the nearby surge protector to cause it to turn off. The monitor went black and every other object that relied on power to function was immediately turned off in the office. "What was that? What in the hell just happened? Why is the computer off? Why in the hell is everything else turned off?" Dad said exasperated.

"Now just calm down, Bob, I'm sure it's just some little glitch," Mom said as she came closer to investigate.

Eventually, Mom found the problem and simply turned the surge protector back on. Soon, everything began to work again except for the equipment, such as the printer, fax, and scanner. Every time Dad clicked the print button on the screen, nothing would print. The fax and scanner did not work either. After about three hours of using unintelligent methods, such as punching the equipment, Dad decided to call the IBM hotline for help. "I knew this computer idea was fucking worthless," Dad grumbled to himself as he dialed the number.

"Hello, you have reached IBM's helpline, this is Lisa speaking," said the IBM tech.

"Yes, my name is Bob Koven with Discovery Zone, Inc. and you guys installed some of your goddamn glorious disasters for me yesterday," Dad yelled.

"I don't believe I'm familiar with that term or tone of voice, sir, but if you'll calm down, I will be glad to help you," Lisa said in a stern voice.

"I'm not going to calm down, goddamn it! Today is the opening day of my business and these fucking machines are broken. They won't do anything. They're just sitting there being worthless and costing me time and money! Lisa, if you don't send one of your goddamn technicians down here in the next few hours, I'm going to throw this goddamn computer equipment into the parking lot! And may I remind you that I have yet to pay for the motherfuckers!"

"Now just calm down, sir! I will try to get the nearest technician to you as soon as possible. What is your location?"

"1321 Pleasant Hill Rd, Duluth, Georgia."

"Alright, Mr. Koven, there should be a representative at your store by noon. However, I can't seem to find you in our computers," Lisa said.

"What do you mean, you can't find me in your computers? I bought eight of the goddamn things!" Dad exaggerated.

"Well, I'm sure I'll find your name eventually. Have a nice day, Mr. Koven."

"I would already have had one if it wasn't for this damn thing," Dad said staring at the computer and its components.

After Dad hung up the phone, he walked out of the office and into the store. He quickly came to a stop when the reality of owning an indoor playground set in. There were kids screaming and running everywhere. Birthday cakes were being dropped, pizzas thrown, cokes spilled, and numerous other chaotic events simultaneously taking place. Just as Dad began to take his next step, a young boy traveling at a relatively high velocity, collided into Dad's right leg. As the boy crashed to the floor he looked up to see Dad saying, "Jesus Christ! Watch where you're going, son!"

The frightened boy quickly ran off without saying a word. Finally, after a few straight hours of intense order-giving to employees to "pick up the goddamn pace!" Dad decided to retire back to his office to try and let his blood pressure come down. As he sat in his chair looking at the immobilized computer machinery, he glanced at his watch and noticed that it was one o'clock and the technician had still not shown up. "This is a goddamn disaster," he said as he made another attempt to print a cost report.

As expected, the attempt failed and Dad did what he does so well-lost his temper. "That's it! I'm going to throw these motherfuckers into the parking lot," he shouted from the office.

At this point, Bobby and I were working behind the redemption counter and could hear Dad's verbal dissatisfaction loud and clear. "Dad sounds pretty mad," Bobby said.

"Yeah, I think the shit's getting ready to hit the fan" We observed Dad suddenly storming out of the office with the massive IBM printer.

"He's looking pretty determined," Bobby said.

"I wouldn't try to stop him," I said watching with amazement.

It was about the time that Jason, the IBM technician, arrived in the parking lot and he was able to observe Dad make a shot put-like throw and land the printer into a nearby handicapped parking space. As Jason stepped out of his car in astonishment, Dad stared back and said, "You're late!"

"You just completely ruined an eight hundred dollar piece of equipment," Jason said in shock.

"I know, and the best part about it is that I haven't paid a dime for it," Dad remarked. "And unless you would like to see one of those precious scanners take flight, I suggest you get your ass in the store and fix the rest of the equipment."

Jason quickly made his way to the store and got to work, with Dad's supervision, of course. After about an hour, Jason installed a few drivers and fixed the problem. Dad quickly thanked Jason, gave him a tip, and said goodbye. After the computer problem had been fixed, Dad decided to lessen the degree of chaos taking place in the store. As his blood pressure began to rise again, he noticed than one of the kids was dragging multiple mousetraps that were stuck on the bottom of his sock. He quickly turned to one of the teenage employees, Stacy, and said, "Jesus Christ, Stacy! Can't you get some of these kids under control? They've gotten into the mousetraps and there are birthday cakes everywhere," Dad said.

"I know, Mr. Koven. They are uncontrollable. One of them even went number two in the ball pen. It's making a horrible smell too," Stacy said.

"Well, clean it up, goddamn it! What in the hell am I paying you for anyway?" Dad yelled.

"Not to clean up shit!" Stacy screamed.

"You're fired, goddamn it!"

"Fine! Find some one else to clean up this shit!" With that Stacy stormed out.

Dad was now extremely overheated and out of patience. Anybody who approached him was either not doing their job right or not doing enough. By the end of the day the entire working force at that particular Discovery Zone became unemployed.

Mom had left much earlier in the day; however, she did return as closing time neared. When she walked into the store she found Dad, Bobby, and me sitting at one of the tables. She looked at the store and then at us with confusion and said, "Where is everyone?"

"He fired them all," Bobby said.

"What!? You fired all of our employees?" Mom said in a shocked voice. "Bob, who in the hell is going to open the goddamn store tomorrow?" she cried.

"I don't know," he said in a tired, defeated voice.

"Jesus Pete! How could you? I don't understand. Who in the hell fires people before they have found a replacement?" Mom said.

"I'll explain it to you on the way home," Dad said as he got up to close the store.

Dad told Mom all that had happened throughout the day in the car on the way home. When we got to our house we went straight to bed.

The only possible lesson that I could find in this fiasco was that when explaining how to operate something, you should be very detailed and informed, because you never know when you are dealing with a Mr. Koven. Maybe one other lesson could be, hire before you fire, or you could be running the show alone.

The One and Only Mr. Harris

I have a theory that every family has one close friend or another whom they love to talk about. Although the thought is that the two friends constantly gossip with each other and about each other on or off the phone, but what really is discussed is the two friends' relationship by their unsuspecting kids. Tim Harris and Dad first met each other over thirty years ago. They were neighbors in their first houses. A week has not passed since that time without a infinitely long telephone call between the two men.

In order to escape the harsh work environment that Monday through Friday encompasses, we often travel to our cabin in the mountains near Highlands, North Carolina. However, Lake Burton is only located a few miles from the traveling route, which happens to be where the Harrises have a great lake house. Because of its strategic location, and the fact that Dad and Mr. Harris might as well have been Siamese twins, we frequently visit them and even spend entire weekends with them from time to time. This is the place where many of my memories blossomed.

It was another exciting Fourth of July weekend at Lake Burton, but as we pulled into the driveway and came to a stop, Dad said, "It's going to be hotter than a furnace in hell in that house."

"Honey, it always is, and you always vow that we'll never be back," Mom chirped.

"What do you expect when they don't turn on the air conditioning," Bobby said.

"That is what I expect. Who in the hell has an air conditioner and doesn't use it in the middle of the summer?" Dad asked.

"It was just the way that Brenda grew up. They didn't have an air conditioner so they just opened the windows."

"So, don't make use of a technological advancement?" I said sarcastically.

"Alright, that's enough. We better get going anyway," Dad said as he noticed Brenda Harris, coming to the front door.

"Hey y'all!" greeted Brenda as she came out of the house.

"Hey!" Mom and Dad replied.

When Brenda Harris came closer and looked at Bobby and me she said, "Hey boys, you guys just go and make yourselves at home. The other boys are out water- skiing right now, but Tim is on the grill if y'all are hungry."

"Thank you," we both said as we headed for the barbecue grill.

It was the same every year. Tim Harris was burning meat on the grill, the five pet dogs were running everywhere, the humidity was unbearable, no air conditioning was turned on, alcohol and finger foods were abundant, Frank Sinatra was being played in the background, and as usual, Bobby and I found ourselves listening to the adult conversation while waiting for the older Harris boys to return. As Bobby and I turned the corner of the house and approached Tim Harris, we noticed he was standing near a brand new silver grill. "Hey, Mr. Harris," I said.

"Hey! Are you guys hungry?" he asked.

"No, we already ate on the way here," we both lied as we noticed one of the chickens catching on fire.

"Well, we have plenty here to eat if you guys do get hungry," he said.

"Thanks," we both said in unison and made our way into the house to look for more edible things to eat.

By the time Bobby and I had found a bag of chips and other snacks, the adults had congregated on the upper deck of the boathouse. Bobby and I went to join the conversation that was taking place. We sat down on some of the patio furniture nearby, when I heard Dad talking about Bennett Hutchinson, another close friend of Dad and Tim Harris.

"I heard that new lake house of his is absolutely amazing," Dad said.

"Yeah, it is nice. But you know, Bob, I believe he actually copied my new additions," Mr. Harris claimed.

"Really?" Dad said with interest.

"Yeah, and not only that, but I think he was just trying to outdo me. He let me finish my renovations first, figure out what he could improve upon and do better, and then built his house bigger and better," Tim Harris said with obvious resentment.

"Well, goddamn. I believe you may be right," Dad said.

"Yeah, no matter what I do, it seems like Bennett has got to do it better or else he isn't happy. It's like that about everything, you know," Harris said.

As Bobby and I sat listening, Bobby remarked, "they sound just like two old complaining women."

"Yeah, really," I said with a laugh.

"Brenda, where is Julianne?" Dad inquired.

"Well, Bob, this morning she was looking at herself in the mirror and said that she was too fat to put her bathing suit on and come outside. I told her that she was being ridiculous. You know she brought her new boyfriend, Steve, up here this weekend. He's such a nice young man. We're kind of hoping that he'll be the one," Brenda said

"That girl! Too fat? That is ridiculous. She's the most in shape thing I've seen," Dad retorted.

"Try telling her that. I think she's also kind of jealous of Jeffrey's new girlfriend, Cara," Brenda said

"Why is that?" Mom asked.

"Well, I know you guys haven't met her yet, but you can't miss her. She has the biggest boobs I have ever seen. They're huge!" Brenda said.

"She's not lying, either," Tim Harris chuckled. "They're so big that Jeffrey and his friends call her Boomer."

"Well, I can't wait to meet her," Dad said as he gazed around.

"How are Russell and Hilary doing?" Mom asked wanting to change the subject.

"They're doing pretty good. Russell has a real good job at the company, and Hilary is selling computers like crazy. She has the leading number of sales of anybody in Georgia," Harris said.

"That's just great. Are they planning on having children soon?" Dad quizzed.

"I don't know, Bob. They're both working pretty hard right now. I think things will just have to calm down before they start a family," Brenda said.

It was about this time that all the younger adults arrived at the lake house in the Mastercraft ski boat. They poured out of the boat and raced into the house. Bobby and I decided to go inside to meet the new girlfriend and greet Russell and Jeff. When we walked into the kitchen, Jeff and Russell saw us and said, "Hey guys. How y'all doing?"

"Pretty good. We were getting tired of listening to the two old men complain, so we decided to come in here," I said.

"Well, tell me when y'all get bored and we'll go tubing or skiing. Bobby, are you up to jumping off The Bridge tonight?" Russell asked.

"Hell, yes!" he replied.

Right then I noticed an attractive girl walking in our direction with Jeff. It was Cara and Brenda Harris had been absolutely right in her description.

"Cara, this is Bobby and Matt Koven," Jeff said with a smile that was obvious.

"Hi, it's nice to meet you," Bobby said as he tried with all of his strength to look into her eyes instead of her chest.

"It's nice to meet you guys, too," Cara said.

Throughout the entire introduction, I had yet to look at her face. I was absolutely blown away and could not regain my composure. As she glanced at me, and when Bobby also noticed my state, he gave me a sharp elbow in the side. When I looked up, I stuttered, "Yes, it's very nice to meet you, too."

As she walked away, Bobby turned to me. "You're pathetic."

"Shut up," I replied.

After five more Frank Sinatra songs had passed by, Russell, Hilary, Jeff, Boomer, their friend Kevin, Julianne, Bobby, and I all headed out on the lake to do some tubing and skiing. The tubing was a lot of fun however, and with Jeffrey Harris behind the wheel I 'm not exactly sure if I would call it tubing because once you reach the 52 mph mark, you are not holding on for fun anymore; you start to hold on for dear life. After tubing, we all headed for The Bridge. Although it is at least forty feet high, it is actually quite fun. Anyway, after a few hours of fun on the lake we all returned to the house for dinner. Dinner was not quite ready, so Bobby and I swam in the lake and relaxed on the chair floats, although it is really quite difficult to relax with all five dogs swimming around you and knocking over the floating coolers. I eventually got out of the lake and went into the house where I found Dad lying on a couch and complaining about his blood pressure.

"It's so goddamn hot in here that I could roast a marshmallow," he said.

"It does seem a little warm. Are you o.k.?" I asked.

"Hell no, I'm not o.k. My blood pressure is through the roof! I feel like a goddamn boiled lobster, and I'm about ready to throw that goddamn Frank Sinatra record out the window."

"Well, do you want me to get you anything?" I asked.

"No. I'll be o.k., but thanks," Dad said as I walked away.

Kevin was in the kitchen making some Summertime Lemonade spiked with vodka that he and Mr. Harris's sons would always lure me into drinking. After everyone had eaten, it was time for the older folks, my parents, and Mr. and Mrs. Harris to leave on the pontoon boat for the fireworks display on the lake. Bobby and I would stay back with the older guys and their friends to watch them launch water balloons at commuting boats of old farts on their way to the fireworks. After launching a balloon into the hull of a passing boat with enough velocity to knock down a brick wall, we decided it was time to leave, especially when we realized that there was a dent the size of a football in the hull of the victimized boat. Next, we proceeded to the fireworks, which were actually amazing for Lake Burton. After this event, the Harris boys decided to take my brother and me on their journey to Tap Time, the only bar on the lake that had lost its liquor license multiple times for serving underage people. I was a seventh grader, and I had never seen so many drunken young kids in my life. Everything was going great until Jeffrey decided to try and hit on one of the girls near the bar. In the midst of his attempt, the girl's monster of a boyfriend approached Jeff and landed a fist right in his face. As if it had been done many times, Jeff's older brother, Russell, quickly confronted the girl's boyfriend with a nice right hook to the jaw. This was the spark that ignited the flame and soon the entire place turned into an all-out brawl. Jeff's good friend, Kevin, stood on top of one of the tables to get a handle on the situation, when to his surprise, the unnoticed ceiling fan smacked him on the back of the head causing him to pass out. Bobby and I took this moment as our cue to get the hell out of there. While Bobby grabbed Kevin, I got Jeff's and Russell's attention and we made for the boat that was docked nearby. We got back to the lake house safely and all was well, at least for us.

Once at the house, I found to my horror that Cara had walked into the bedroom not knowing that my naked father had been sleeping there and proceeded to get into one of the bunk beds. In a somewhat drunken state and suffering from heat exhaustion, he had passed out in the buff. I believe that this event may have traumatized her for life.

"Jeffrey, is that you?" she said as she slipped into the bed.

"What in the…" Dad was saying as he rolled over to see who it was.

"Oh my god! Is that you, Mr. Koven?" Cara was in shock.

"Who in the hell do you think it is? What's wrong? Have you never seen a naked fat man before?" Dad exclaimed while not even attempting to grab a cover.

"No!" she screamed and she ran out of the room. Cara continued yelling, "Mr. Koven's naked in there!"

Julianne quickly said, "O-o-o, you saw Mr. Koven naked?"

"Yes," Cara said.

"My god, the girl will be blinded for life," Mr. Harris joked.

"Shut the hell up, you asshole," Dad shouted from the room.

"Just go back to bed, you old fart. You should consider yourself lucky that anybody but Gale would come close to your bed!" Harris called back.

Weekends spent at the Harris lake house were definitely weekends to be remembered. There were always too many people for the number of beds available, but no one really minded, particularly adults, who were always too tired to care.

Losing Pounds and Euros

Following the trip to Spain, it took four more years for everyone to get up enough courage to plan another trip to Europe. After my hellish junior year of high school and Bobby's stellar junior year at Dartmouth College, we decided to take a ten-day family journey through England, Germany, Austria, Hungary, and Ireland. Moreover, we would not be traveling alone, but would enjoy our European experience with the Keeter family. Our past our trips with the Keeter family have always led to a single destination where warm weather, golf courses, pools, and other amenities were plentiful. However, I could already foresee that a grueling, non-stop, professionally guided tour by Dad, the tour guide that knows something about everything, might cause a few problems.

"Is everything packed in the car?" Dad yelled from his bedroom as we prepared to leave for the airport.

"Yes, everything is packed," I said.

"Have the dogs been fed?" he asked.

"They've been fed. Dad, have you arranged for someone to feed the dogs while we are gone?" I asked.

My question must have sparked some consideration because Dad soon asked, "Gale! Have you arranged for someone to feed the dogs while we're gone?"

"Yes dear, I always have Chris, the next door neighbor's son, take care of it. You need to remember to pay him when we get back," Mom replied from another room. Dad never answered.

I sat on the living room couch waiting, as usual, for everyone else. Mom came downstairs toting a camera. She had that flustered look on her face that she always has during stressful situations.

"Mom, I think you need to relax. You look like we're all going to die."

"Well, I just know that we're going to forget something. Your father is so goddamn hard to travel with."

"Gale! Have you seen my wallet? I can't find it anywhere!" his request came from the bedroom.

"I haven't seen it! Look in your pants' pockets!" Mom yelled back.

"I already looked there, goddamn it!" Came the furious response.

"He is so disorganized," Mom complained just as Dad walked into the living room.

"I've lost it. I've lost my fucking wallet thirty minutes before we have to be at the airport!" Dad was in a panic.

"Bob, how in the hell could you have lost your wallet? Are you that dumb? It has all of your credit cards, photo ID, and money!" Mom was livid.

Dad thought for a moment. "I must have left it on the counter at Starbucks this morning."

"Why were you at Starbucks? You're supposed to be on a diet, and don't give me that bullshit about how you ordered one of those gay, vanilla soy non-fat pieces of shit because I know that you go in there and just eat chocolate." Mom was on a roll now.

"Wait just a goddamn minute!" Dad interjected.

I entered the polite discussion. "Would you guys shut the hell up! "Maybe we could save the diet bullshit for later, and start looking for Dad's wallet since we have to leave in five minutes."

We all split up and began tearing the entire house apart in search of the elusive wallet and the fifteen hundred dollars of cash that was in it. Not finding the wallet, Dad made some quick phone calls to American Express and Visa in order to cancel the credit cards. We loaded into the packed Suburban and Dad laid rubber, leaving our two dogs behind in the driveway wondering what in the hell had just happened.

Dad's cell phone began to ring as we barreled down the wrong side of the road in order to cut off a line of traffic. "Hello," Dad said in an angry voice.

"Hey, gang!" screeched Grandma from the cell phone.

"Jesus Christ, Sue, I can't talk now! I've lost my goddamn wallet and we're late for the plane," Dad yelled into the phone.

"Now Bob, we both know that each of us is a diabetic and when we get a little grumpy, eating a cracker never hurts," Grandma preached.

As Dad rolled his eyes, he looked at Mom and said, "Would you please talk to your mother? She's going off on that feed me a cracker bullshit." Although Dad was already extremely angry about the present situation, things got worse when a Hummer 2 pulled in front of us and blocked our lane. With cell phone in hand, Dad shifted into first gear, floored the accelerator, and steered the Suburban over the nearby sidewalk. The impact of the random objects that we bounced over threw the luggage that I took such care to pack into the air all around the inside of the car. "We're going to be late as goddamn last year's Christmas!" Dad launched the cell phone at the passenger window. I can still see the look on his face as he watched the phone sail out the window not realizing that it was open, and hearing grandma's voice trailing away as the phone left our vehicle.

"Are you crazy?" Mom screamed.

"Listen, enough has already gone wrong for an entire trip, so just stop yelling and calm down," Dad requested.

"You" want "me" to calm down?" Mom replied. "Bob, you're the psycho who thinks throwing phones out the goddamn window is better than simply hanging up on a person."

"All right, guys, that's enough," I said. "You both need to calm down before we reach Hanover to pick up Bobby, or else this whole trip will be an absolute disaster." I knew if anyone could aggravate Dad the most, it is the one person who is exactly like him, Bobby. We arrived at the airport and Dad drove through the grass in order to save time and avoid the automatic security points on the way to our friends' airplane hangar.

Once the pilots secured the bags on the plane, Mr. Keeter, and the three Kovens made ourselves comfortable for the journey to Hanover, New Hampshire. After picking up Bobby, we would fly to Gander, Newfoundland to clear our passports, and then fly to London where we would meet up with Mrs. Keeter and Kaylan who had been in London for the previous five days.

We landed in New Hampshire and Bobby was standing outside of the small terminal. I noticed my parents excited look as we approached him.

"Hey, honey! It's so nice to see you again," Mom said, embracing him with a big hug.

"Hey, Sport! You look good, maybe a little broken out, but you look good," Dad said happily.

"Thanks, Dad, it's great to see you, too." Bobby rolled his eyes.

"He is not broken out, Bob," Mom said reassuringly. "Don't listen to him, he can't even remember where he placed his wallet," she said to Bobby.

"Are you serious?" Bobby was stunned.

"Yeah, all his credit cards, driver's license, not to mention fifteen hundred bucks in cash are all gone," I said.

"That's horrible," Bobby said as we made our way back to the airplane.

Once the pilots secured Bobby's luggage we were off to Gander. Roughly two hours later, Dad stepped off the plane looking as if he owned it and made his way to the small terminal. We all followed him into the terminal, which was a small, ugly gray building. However, inside the terminal was quit pleasant. Bottles of local maple syrups lined the tops of random pieces of furniture while pictures accompanied by interesting facts about Newfoundland lined the walls. A table held a variety of complimentary foods including ice creams, muffins, chocolates, granola bars, fruits, soft drinks, and bottled water. The woman working in the facility was very hospitable and happy to entertain all of Dad's questions.

"Hi, I'm Bob Koven," Dad said as to her.

"It's nice to meet you, my name is Sara." She had a Canadian accent,

"So, how many flights come through here in a day?" Dad asked as he browsed around the main room while slyly making his way toward the complimentary ice cream.

"It really depends. Some days we have corporate jets flying in and out non-stop and other days there's not much traffic at all," Sara said.

"This food looks great! Do you ever offer dinner or anything like that to people traveling through?" Dad asked.

"All the time. We fix lobster dinners for lots of celebrities that come through here," Sara said.

"That sounds like a great idea! We'll be coming back through here in about ten days. I can't think of anything better than fresh lobster after being stuck on an airplane for four hours," Dad said while grinning. Once everyone had visited the rest rooms and our passports were cleared, we were on our way to England.

It was about 7:00 a.m. when we arrived in London and everyone was a little jet lagged. Thirty minutes later we met Mrs. Keeter and Kaylan in the lobby of the Stafford Hotel.

"Hey Bobby! How are you?" Mrs. Keeter asked in her high-pitched voice as she gave, Bobby, the first one into the lobby, a hug.

"I'm doing pretty well," Bobby said and saw Kaylan and gave her a hug.

"Are you real tired?" Kaylan asked.

"Not at all. I've only had about ten hours of sleep over the past four days because of exams."

As we filed into the lobby, I notice that our conversation seemed to be abnormally loud, and that everyone else in the lobby was speaking quite softly. All I could hear was Dad raving about how wonderful the flight was and I saw him tipping the bellhops too many pounds, mistaking the currency for dollars.

"Julie, there is no better way to travel. We had such a great flight, and you would have loved the terminal in Gander," Dad exclaimed.

"Dad, why is everyone here speaking so quiet? It's kind of strange," I said, looking around.

"Well, Matt, that's the way they speak over here. You are used to loud obnoxious Americans like your brother. By the way, that is a good observation. You should inform your loud brother so he quits making a fool of himself," Dad said and walked over to the check-in counter.

Mrs. Keeter informed everyone that a tour bus ride was in store for us in the following morning and that there was nothing planned for the remainder of the day. Therefore, everyone had something light to eat, went into their rooms, and took a nap for a few hours. We spent the rest of the day relaxing and discovering the immediate area around our hotel.

The telephone rang. "Hello," I said as I picked up the phone.

"Good morning, Mr. Koven. It is seven thirty and this is your wake-up call," said the voice on the other end of the line.

"Thank you," I groaned. "Rise and shine, fat man!" I yelled to Bobby who was in the other queen size bed.

"What time is it?" Bobby asked.

"It's seven thirty and we gotta get going. God forbid we miss the Big Red Bus Tour."

"The Big Red what Tour?" Bobby whined.

"It's just a big bus that drives you around the city to see the famous landmarks. Anyway, get your ass up because we only have about forty-five minutes to get showered and eat breakfast," I said.

The telephone rang. It was Koven senior.

"Hey, buddy! Are y'all awake?"

"Yeah, we had a wake-up call.

"Good. Hurry up because we're having breakfast at a restaurant called Riccalou. It's about a quarter of a mile from here. We'll barely have time, but I think it will work," Dad said.

"O.k.. We'll be there." I knew the strain on time would not be a problem for me and Bobby, but I wasn't too sure about everyone else. The Keeters had been up since 7:00, and were just beginning to browse the room service menu when the phone rang. Jim Keeter picked it up.

"Morning, Jim, hope I didn't wake you," Dad said.

"No, Julie and I were already awake and getting ready."

"Well, listen, I was down here in the lobby and the concierge said there's this great little restaurant called Riccalou right up the street. He said they serve a great quick breakfast and I though since we are walking in that direction to begin with, it would be a good place to eat."

"You know, we'll only have thirty minutes to eat and we still have to get there," Keeter said trying to discourage Dad.

"Yeah, that's why Gale and I are leaving now to save us a table and get started," Dad assured.

"O.k.. We'll try to make it," Keeter said.

Mom and Dad quickly left the hotel and began walking toward the restaurant. "Bob, I'm not sure if it's such a good idea to be rushing Jim around like this. You know he hates to be rushed," Mom cautioned.

"Don't worry, there's no rush at all, honey. Besides now we'll already be closer to the bus stop."

"You know where the bus stop is?" Mom asked.

"No, Julie just told me that it was on Piccadilly Street in this direction," Dad said.

Eventually everyone made it to Riccalou, though Jim did not look too happy. The service at the restaurant was superb and we were on our way to the bus stop in about thirty minutes. After walking for about fifteen minutes and watching some of the buses pass by without stopping, Dad asked, "What's that bus say on the side?"

"The Original Bus Tour," Kaylan said.

"I keep seeing the Big Red Buses pass by, but only the Original Bus Tour buses are stopping," Dad announced.

"Yes, but we definitely need to get on the Big Red Bus Tour because that's the one that was recommended to me," Julie Keeter said.

After walking another five minutes and trying to chase down Big Red Bus Tour buses, Bobby turned to me and said, "What the fuck's the difference? The Original Bus Tour seems to have more stops and has red buses too. I say we just take the Original Bus Tour."

"Just try and find a Big Red Bus, bus stop," I said.

"This is fucking ridiculous," Bobby muttered.

"Juulllieee," Jim whined. "Are you sure that you know where the Big Red Bus stops? I thought you had everything planned out?"

Julie ignored everyone's comments while she and everyone else searched for the bus stop. Finally, after looking down another street we found a bus stop and bought tickets for the tour. Within five minutes, a bus stopped by and picked us up. When we stepped on the bus, the driver handed us each a pair of earphones to listen to the guided tour. We made our way to the upper deck of the bus and found that the only seats that were empty were randomly scattered from the front to the back. So, everyone found a seat and made themselves comfortable for the time being. However, we were not comfortable for long.

By the time the bus had moved about a block, Dad looked down at his watch and realized that the changing of the guard at Buckingham Palace was going to take place in ten minutes. Dad knew we would miss the event if we stayed on the bus, so he jumped up and hollered, "Guys, we gotta go, we gotta go! The Changing of the Guard is in ten minutes. Let's go!" Everyone on the bus looked somewhat confused, but not knowing what else to do, we all jumped up and hurried to the lower deck. Dad had the bus driver stop the bus and we got off. "Alright, Buckingham Palace is that way," Dad said, pointing down the street.

"Bob, you're right that Buckingham Palace is that way, but it is three miles that way!" Mom shouted.

"Gale, would you be quiet and go!" Dad commanded.

We all started walking toward the palace at an accelerated pace. After a few minutes, we were walking fast enough to break a sweat. Perspiration began to drip down Dad's face and I could tell that the tension level was rising with every step. Suddenly, Dad flagged down a taxi and it came to a stop.

The female cab driver quickly rolled down her window as she saw Dad trying to say something. "How many people can you take?" he asked.

"I'm only allowed to take five," the woman replied.

"Can you fit two extra?" Dad stated emphatically.

"No, five is the legal limit," the woman replied.

"Damn! All right, Matt get into the car!" Dad ordered.

"No, there's not enough room for everyone," I protested.

Dad looked at me angrily and then directed his attention to Bobby and said, "Bobby, get into the car!" Bobby repeated my excuse. Dad, now beginning to feel a little embarrassed, looked at Mom and ordered, "Gale, would you get into the goddamn cab? Please!"

"Bob, there will not be enough room for all of us," Mom said.

"Gale, if you don't get in this car right now, I'm gonna kick your ass!"

Mom shot Dad an angry look and said, "Well then go ahead and do it. There is no way that I am going to simply leave Jim and Julie. If you want to take a taxi, then go ahead!" Mom turned around, and continued walking in the direction of Buckingham Palace.

"Fine! I'll take the dammed cab!" Dad shouted and got into the taxi.

"I don't know about you, but I'm not going to miss a free ride," Bobby said jumping in alongside Dad. I convinced myself that Bobby had a good point, so I jumped into the car behind him. The driver looked a little shocked, but said, she had seen it all and not to worry about it.

Kaylan had joined her parents, who had been walking slightly ahead of our fiasco and us. They tried to ignore the confrontation as best as possible; however, when Mom caught up with them with a determined look on her face, Julie said, "You go, girlfriend!"

Dad, Bobby, and I made it to Buckingham Palace in time. We fought our way to the front of the crowd, and once we found a decent position, we waited. Soon, the music began to play and Dad said, "They should have taken the cab. Looks like they're going to miss everything."

At the moment that Dad's words trailed off, he felt someone poke him in the back and say jokingly, "I'm going to kick your ass!"

Dad whirled around to find Mom and the Keeters standing behind him. Everyone had laughed and Dad cooled off. After viewing the changing of the guard, we finished the rest of the Big Red Bus Tour, and headed back to the hotel. The next two days in London were spent shopping and enjoying other tours of some of the many amazing London sights.

We spent the following seven days visiting monument after monument in Munich, Salzburg, Vienna, Budapest, and Shannon. Surprisingly, Dad was able to control himself for the rest of the time, even when tension was high.

We arrived home exhausted and ready for a rest. Following a late and restful morning the next day, I happened to notice something in the middle of the basement hallway. As I approached the object, it took the shape of Dad's missing wallet. In the middle of the hallway! I had mixed feelings of surprise, relief, and annoyance. I quickly ran up stairs to inform everyone the great news.

"Dad! I found your wallet," I exclaimed.

"Oh my god! Where in the world was it?"

"In the middle of the basement hallway," I said. Dad looked at me with astonishment.

"Well Matt, thank you," he said with a reserved look as he held out his hand.

The finding of Dad's wallet only served to lighten his mood and increase his appreciation for my awareness. Overall, this vacation proved that Dad is actually able to relax and enjoy a trip, being the most recent; I think it will be the beginning of a new trend in his behavior. Well, that's the hope anyway.

0-595-33216-1

Made in the USA
Columbia, SC
27 March 2024

33716731R00081